Acid Reflux

Eating for Relief

Table of Contents

Why the Acid Reflux Diet?

Foods to Avoid

Lettuce Nut Salad

Olive Tapenade

Creamy "Cheesy" Broccoli Soup

Kelp Noodle Stir-Fry

Veggie Burger

Crispy Fish Sandwich with Quick Slaw

Grain-Free Soft Burger Buns

Chicken Tenders

Soft Baked Pretzel

Sausage Stuffed "Corn" Muffin

Chicken and Waffles

Sweet Potatoes Roast

Red Pepper Crab Soup

Chicken and "Rice"

Dinner

Coconut Chicken Bites

Cashew Chicken

Korean Beef

Chicken and Dumplings

Chicken & Berry Salsa

Roasted Turkey Legs

Herb Crusted Pork Chops with Cinnamon Apples

Ground Meat Stuffed Peppers

Beef Pot Roast

Pork Butt Roast

Garlic and White Wine Steamed Mussels

Macadamia Crusted Ahi Tuna

Parchment Baked Salmon

Smoked Salmon Eggs Benedict

Almond Crusted Pan Seared Scallops

Crunchy Cashew Chicken

Sautéed Mongolian Beef

Grain-Free Chicken and Waffles

Healthy Chicken Pie

Mirepoix with Red Sauce

Nuts & Turkey Burgers

Natural Italian Chicken Sausage

Herb Roasted Pork Tenderloin

Slow Cooker Herbed Chicken

Oysters and Pancetta Gratin

Seafood Paella

Asian Empanada

Smoked Salmon Avocado Salad

Sliced Veggies With Chicken

No-Crust Kale Quiche

Snacks

Broccoli Fries

Nuts & Raisin Bars

Simple Almond Apricot Balls

Prosciutto Wrapped Dates

Sweet Cinnamon Pretzel

Green Deviled Eggs 'N Ham

Baked Sweet Plantains

Honey Nut Bun

Coconut Macaroons

Onion Crumpets

Apple Bread

Fruit and Nut Apricot Pockets

Green Baked Avocado

Delicious Apple Smoothie

Crispy Kale Chips

Almond Butter Crunch Granola Bar

Chicks in a Blanket

Coconut Crisps

Apple Dump Muffins

Ants On A Log

Piña Colada Smoothie

Awesome Strawberry Chia Pudding

Hearty Apple Almond Salad

Spinach Mushroom Muffins

Tahini Evening Snack

Frozen Cashew Balls

Flourless Cocoa Zucchini Muffin

Chocolate Chip Trail Mix

Vanilla Bean Shortbread Cookies

Crunchy Eggplant Chips with Honey

Why the Acid Reflux Diet?

Gastroesophageal reflux disease (GERD), also known as acid reflux or heartburn, is a pretty common medical condition which causes stomach acid and/or bile to travel back up the esophagus and mouth. Normally, a small valve located at the end of the esophagus (where it connects to the stomach) prevents stomach acid and partially digested food from coming back up. However, some people have a weaker valve or their valve does not close properly, allowing the contents of the stomach to enter the esophagus.

Because stomach acid is extremely strong, it can damage the delicate esophagus and mouth tissues which are not designed to withstand assault from such an acidic substance. Stomach acid that ends up in the mouth can also damage teeth. If you suffer from GERD, you may notice this reflux, which feels like an unpleasant burning sensation in your chest and throat.

Common remedies for GERD include antacids made from aluminum, calcium, magnesium and/or bicarbonates. These substances neutralize acid, preventing it from damaging exposed tissues. However, using antacids in excess can cause ion and mineral imbalances in the body, and most are very hard on the kidneys. A better solution is to control acid reflux with diet and lifestyle.

The GERD Diet focuses on greatly reducing or eliminating many "problem" foods that trigger GERD in many people. Everyone is different, and your trigger foods may not be the same as someone else's. For this reason, there is no universal GERD diet. However, some foods are known to be irritating to a large amount of GERD sufferers. These "problem" foods include many fats, spices, stimulants and acidic foods. You will need to experiment in order to find your personal triggers, but the next page will give you general guidelines in regards to the majority of people.

For the recipes suggested in this book, choose low-fat cuts of meat (or trim visible fat) and avoid sprinkling with black pepper or other condiments from the list of foods to avoid. If making roast chicken or turkey, you'll usually want to avoid eating the skin. Of course, some recipes call for a squirt of lemon juice or a teaspoon of vinegar. This should not be a problem for most people, as the acidity is dissolved within the rest of the recipe, but if your GERD flares up after such a meal, you may want to consider leaving the offending ingredient out next time.

Foods to Avoid

You will usually want to avoid:

- Acidic fruits and veggies (tomatoes, oranges, lemons, grapefruits, cranberries, as well as their juices)
- Strong-tasting vegetables (raw onions, radishes, hot peppers)
- Fatty meat (regular ground beef, meat with visible fat, bacon, spicy buffalo wings, fried meat such as chicken nuggets)
- Anything fried or extremely fatty (fried mozzarella sticks, French fries, croissants and pastries, battered fish, mayonnaise)
- High-fat dairy (whole milk, ice cream, chocolate milk, regular cheese, cream)
- Caffeine, alcohol and carbonated drinks (soda, carbonated water, carbonated juice, spritzers)
- Spicy or acidic foods (vinegar, chili powder and sauce, black pepper, strong mustard, horseradish, curry, pickles, mint)

Lunch

Red Pepper with Chicken Toppings

Prep time: 15 minutes

Cook time: 15 minutes

Serves: 2

INGREDIENTS

Pizza

1 red pepper

1 yellow pepper

1 small red onion

1 low-sodium cooked organic grass-fed chicken sausage link

1 cup broccoli florets

1 tbsp extra virgin olive oil

Pesto

1 packed cup fresh basil

¼ cup extra virgin olive oil

¼ cup walnuts

3 cloves garlic

¼ tsp Celtic sea salt

INSTRUCTIONS

1. Cut the peppers in half. Remove the stems, cores and seeds. Line a baking sheet with aluminum foil and place the peppers in it skin side up. Put peppers under the broiler and leave them there until the skin has begun to turn black and shriveled.

2. Remove peppers from oven, place in a plastic bag and place in refrigerator until cool.

3. Peel the skins off the peppers and throw them away.

4. Slice the onion into half-moon slices and slice the chicken sausage link into twelve thin slices. Place the onion, sausage slices and broccoli florets with 1 tbsp extra virgin olive oil in a saucepan over medium heat for 4 minutes until vegetables are tender crisp and meat is slightly browned.

5. Place all the pesto ingredients in a food processor and blend until smooth.

6. Put two halves of roasted pepper on a dish, one red and one yellow, open side up. Using a spoon, spread pesto evenly inside each pepper half. Evenly distribute broccoli, onion, and sausage over the tops.

7. Serve.

Quick Pepper Quiche

Prep time: 5 minutes

Cook time: 3-6 minutes

INGREDIENTS

2 cage-free eggs

1 small onion

1 clove garlic

½ red bell pepper

1 tbsp extra virgin olive oil

¼ tsp smoked paprika

INSTRUCTIONS

1. Finely chop onion, garlic and red bell pepper.
2. Pour extra virgin olive oil into a pan over medium heat.
3. Crack eggs and pour into a small bowl. Combine with onion, garlic and red bell pepper and whisk until mixed together.
4. Pour contents of bowl into pan and add smoked paprika. Scramble until desired doneness.
5. Serve.

Sweet Chicken Salad

Prep time: 24 hours (date syrup is created overnight)

Cook time: 50 minutes

Servings: 4

INGREDIENTS

Date Syrup

1 cup water

1 cup pitted dates

Salad

4 pieces grass-fed chicken thighs, coarsely chopped

1 tbsp extra virgin olive oil

7 oz bag Romaine lettuce

1 red bell pepper

1 yellow bell pepper

½ cup walnuts

1 cup strawberries

1 cup kiwi

INSTRUCTIONS

1. For Date Syrup, split the dates down the middle, remove the pits, and place in a bowl with 1 cup water. Place this mixture in the fridge overnight. Stir occasionally if you are able to.

2. Preheat oven to 375. Take the chopped chicken thighs and coat them in olive oil. Place them on a baking dish, cover with aluminum foil, and place them in the oven for 30 minutes.

3. Chop the peppers and slice the strawberries and kiwi.

4. When the chicken has cooked for 30 minutes, remove the aluminum foil and cook for another 15 minutes. After 15 minutes, drizzle half the date syrup mixture over the chicken and cook another 5 minutes.

5. Place the romaine lettuce, peppers, walnuts, strawberries and kiwis in a bowl and toss.

6. Remove chicken from oven and place into the bowl. Drizzle the remaining date syrup over the finished dish and toss.

7. Serve immediately or chill 20 minutes and serve.

Easy Baked Chicken

Prep time: 10 minutes

Cook time: 25 minutes

Serves: 4

INGREDIENTS

4 pieces grass-fed chicken thighs

4 cloves garlic

4 stems rosemary

3 tbsp extra-virgin olive oil

1 lemon

½ cup organic chicken stock

INSTRUCTIONS

1. Preheat oven to 450 degrees.
2. Strip the leaves from the rosemary and crush the garlic. Grate the lemon into zest and juice and separate the two.
3. Place chicken on a baking dish. Add garlic, rosemary, lemon zest, and olive oil. Toss chicken to coat thoroughly and roast (uncovered) 20 minutes.
4. After 20 minutes of roasting, add chicken broth and lemon juice. Turn over chicken.
5. Return to oven, turn oven off and let sit 5 minutes longer.
6. Remove from oven and place on serving dish, pouring pan juices over the chicken. Serve immediately or chill 20 minutes and serve.

Butternut Squash Soup

Prep Time: 10 minutes

Cook Time: 1 hour

Servings: 4

INGREDIENTS

1 medium-large butternut squash (about 2 cups diced)

2 cups chicken stock (or veggie stock)

1/2 cup coconut milk (optional)

1/2 onion (white, yellow or sweet)

1/2 large carrot

1/2 celery stalk

1/2 teaspoon ground coriander (optional)

1 cinnamon stick

Celtic sea salt, to taste

2 tablespoons shelled pumpkin seeds (toasted or raw)

2 tablespoons ghee (or coconut oil or bacon fat)

2 tablespoons coconut oil (or bacon fat)

INSTRUCTIONS

1. Heat oven to 375 degrees F. Heat medium cast iron pan over medium-high heat. Add fat to hot oiled pan.

2. Peel squash and remove seeds. Dice and add to hot oiled pan with salt, to taste. Sauté until golden, about 3 - 4 minutes. Place pan in oven and roast until browned on all sides, about 15 minutes.

3. Heat medium pot over medium-low heat. Add coconut oil to hot pot.

4. Peel and dice onion, celery and carrot. Add to hot oiled pot with cinnamon stick, salt and pepper to taste. Sauté until soft but not browned, about 10 minutes.

5. Remove squash from oven and let cool slightly. Add food processor or high-speed blender and process until puréed.

6. Add chicken broth and coriander (optional) to pot. Increase heat to medium and bring to boil. Simmer about 5 minutes.

7. Stir in squash purée and simmer about 10 minutes. Discard cinnamon stick.

8. Add mixture to food processor or high-speed blender and purée until smooth. Or blend with immerse or stick blender until smooth.

9. Transfer mixture back to hot pot and stir in coconut milk (optional). Transfer to serving dish.

10. Sprinkle with pumpkin seeds and cracked black pepper. Serve hot.

Simple Chicken Matzo Ball Soup

Prep Time: 15 minutes*

Cook Time: 30 minutes

Servings: 4

INGREDIENTS

16 oz (1 lb) chicken pieces

2 cups chicken stock (or vegetable stock)

1 cup almond flour

2 cage-free egg yolks

3/4 teaspoon Celtic sea salt

INSTRUCTIONS

1. In a medium mixing bowl, beat eggs and salt until light and frothy, about 2 minutes. Sift almond flour into bowl and mix until dough comes together.

2. *Cover dough with parchment, if preferred, and refrigerate 2 - 4 hours.

3. Heat medium pot over medium heat. Add 1 teaspoon salt to large pot of water and bring to boil.

4. Place chicken in hot pot skin-side down. Brown chicken on all sides, about 15 minutes.

5. Remove dough from refrigerator and roll into balls. Carefully place dough balls in boiling water. Reduce heat to low, cover and simmer 20 minutes, until cooked through.

6. Add chicken too browned chicken stock. Cook about 15 minutes. Remove chicken and chop, then add back to pot.

7. Transfer matzo balls to serving dish with slotted spoon. Ladle heated chicken stock over matzo balls and serve hot.

Spinach Artichoke Soup

Prep Time: 5 minutes

Cook Time: 30 minutes

Servings: 4

INGREDIENTS

2 cups vegetable broth (or chicken broth)

1 can (13.5 oz) full-fat coconut milk

4 cups spinach leaves

1 1/2 cups artichoke hearts (canned or jarred, drained)

1/2 small onion (yellow or white)

1 garlic clove

2 teaspoons Celtic sea salt

1 tablespoon ghee (or bacon fat or coconut oil)

INSTRUCTIONS

1. Heat medium pot over medium heat. Add fat to hot pot.
2. Peel and thinly slice onion. Peel and finely grate or mince garlic. Add to hot oiled pot and sauté until tender and translucent, about 5 minutes.
3. Fill pot with spinach and stir to wilt. Continue until all spinach is added. Stir in salt.
4. Chop artichoke hearts and add to pot with veggie broth and coconut milk. Stir to combine.
5. Bring to simmer and heat through, about 8 - 10 minutes.
6. Transfer to serving dish and serve hot.

Cream of Mushroom Soup

Prep Time: 5 minutes

Cook Time: 30 minutes

Servings: 4

INGREDIENTS

3 cups vegetable broth (or chicken broth)

1 can (13.5 oz) full-fat coconut milk

4 cups mushrooms (white, baby bella, etc.)

1/2 onion (yellow or white)

1 garlic clove

2 teaspoons Celtic sea salt

2 tablespoons ghee (or bacon fat or coconut oil)

INSTRUCTIONS

1. Heat large pot over medium-high heat. Add 1 tablespoon fat to hot pot.
2. Slice 1 cup mushrooms and add to pot. Sauté until lightly browned and tender, about 5 minutes. Remove from pot and set aside.
3. Add remaining fat to hot pot. Reduce heat to medium.
4. Peel and chop onions and garlic. Add to hot oiled pot and sauté until fragrant and lightly browned, about 5 minutes.
5. Add whole mushrooms to pot and sauté until lightly browned and tender, about 8 - 10 minutes.
6. Transfer mushrooms, onion and garlic to food processor or high-speed blender with vegetable broth, coconut milk and salt. Process until smooth, about 1 - 2 minutes.

7. Or add vegetable broth, coconut milk, salt and pepper to pot and purée with immersion blender.

8. Heat pot over medium heat. Add reserved sliced mushrooms to pot and stir to combine.

9. Bring to simmer and heat through, about 8 - 10 minutes.

10. Transfer to serving dish and serve hot.

Stewed Chicken and Dumplings

Prep Time: 10 minutes

Cook Time: 1 hour 20 minutes

Servings: 4

INGREDIENTS

2 lb whole chicken (innards removed)

6 - 10 cups water

3 carrots

3 celery stalks

1 small white onion (or yellow onion)

4 bay leaves

1 1/2 tablespoons dried thyme (or 4 sprigs fresh thyme)

1/2 teaspoon dried oregano

1 teaspoon paprika

1 tablespoon Celtic sea salt

Dumplings

3 cups almond flour

1/2 cup arrowroot powder

2 cage-free egg

1/2 cup coconut oil, chilled (or coconut or cacao butter, room temperature)

1/2 teaspoon baking soda

1/4 teaspoon ground bay leaf

1 teaspoon dried thyme

1/2 teaspoon ground white pepper (or ground black pepper)

1 teaspoon Celtic sea salt

Nut milk (or chicken broth or stock)

INSTRUCTIONS

1. Heat large pot over medium-high heat. Place chicken breast-down in hot pot. Sear chicken and turn to brown and render out fat for about 15 minutes.

2. Chop carrots and celery. Peel onion and mince. Add to chicken with salt and spices. Sauté about 2 minutes.

3. Add enough water to pot to cover chicken. Increase heat to high and bring to a boil. Reduce heat to medium and simmer about 30 minutes. Place lid loosely over pot to prevent splatter, if necessary.

4. For *Dumplings*, sift almond flour and arrowroot into medium mixing bowl. Cut in solid oil or butter with fork until crumbly mixture forms. Add egg, salt and spices, baking soda, and enough nut milk or chicken broth from pot to bring together soft, slightly sticky dough.

5. Carefully remove chicken from pot with long utensil and set aside. Use utensils to remove skin from chicken. Carve chicken into desired pieces and place back in back.

6. Use spoon or scoop to gently drop dough into pot. Cover with well fitting lid and let simmer about 15 - 20 minutes, until *Dumplings* and chicken are cooked through. Gently stir soup to periodically prevent *Dumplings* from sticking. Turn over any *Dumplings* that are not submerged.

7. Remove from heat and transfer to serving dish. Serve hot.

Chicken Noodle Soup

Prep Time: 10 minutes

Cook Time: 20 minutes

Servings: 2

INGREDIENTS

Noodles

1/2 cup almond flour

1/2 cup arrowroot powder

1/2 cup tapioca flour

1 egg

2 egg yolks

1 tablespoon coconut oil

1/2 teaspoon sea salt

Soup

8 oz skin-on chicken

1 1/2 cup chicken broth or stock

1/2 cup water

2 carrots

1 celery stalk

2 teaspoons dried thyme (4 teaspoons fresh thyme)

Pinch sea salt

INSTRUCTIONS

1. Heat medium pot over medium-high heat. Place chicken skin-side down in hot pot. Sear and render out fat for about 5 minutes.

2. Dice carrots and celery. Add to chicken with salt.

3. Turn chicken and brown on flesh side about 5 minutes. Stir veggies as well.

4. Add thyme, chicken stock and water, and increase heat to high. Bring soup to simmer. Adjust heat as necessary and keep at simmer or soft boil.

5. For *Noodles*, sift almond flour, tapioca flour, 1/3 cup arrow powder and salt into medium mixing bowl. Make well in the center of flour mixture and add egg and yolks. Whisk eggs into flour in circular motion with a fork until dough pulls together.

6. Dust cutting board with half of remaining arrowroot powder. Turn dough out onto cutting board and knead for 5 minutes, until smooth.

7. Add 1 tablespoon coconut oil if dough is too dry. Add 1 tablespoon almond flour at a time if dough is too moist or sticky.

8. Dust cutting board with remaining arrowroot powder. Roll dough into rectangular shape with a rolling pin to about 1/8 inch thickness. Cut pasta sheet into long strips with pizza cutter or sharp knife. Or run past through pasta machine several times until desired thickness is reached. Then use cutting attachment to cut pasta into preferred style.

9. Separate noodles a bit and place gently in simmering soup for about 3 minutes.

10. Transfer to serving dish and serve immediately.

Chicken Patties

Prep Time: 5 minutes

Cook Time: 10 minutes

Servings: 2

INGREDIENTS

8 oz chicken

1 egg

1/4 cup coconut flour

1/2 sweet onion

1 tablespoon apple cider vinegar

1 teaspoon sea salt

1 teaspoon paprika

1 teaspoon ground sage

1 teaspoon dried thyme

1 teaspoon fennel seed (optional)

1/2 teaspoon nutmeg (optional)

1 tablespoon water

Coconut oil (for cooking)

INSTRUCTIONS

1. Heat medium skillet over medium heat and lightly coat with coconut oil.

2. Grind chicken meat and peeled 1/2 onion to medium grind in food processor, bullet blender, or meat grinder. Or grind onion alone and add to pre-ground chicken in medium bowl.

3. Add apple cider vinegar, spices and 1 tablespoon coconut flour to ground chicken and onion. Mix well until combined. Form into 2 large or 4 small patties and place on plate.

4. Beat egg with water and pour egg wash over patties. Gently flip patties to get them evenly covered with egg wash. Take coconut flour and sprinkle over both sides of egg washed patties. Pat coconut flour gently into patties.

5. Place coated patties into hot oiled skillet and cook about 3 - 4 minutes, until golden brown and crisp. Flip and cook another 3 - 4 minutes, or until done.

6. Remove cooked patties from pan and drain on paper towel. Serve hot.

Crab Cakes

Prep Time: 5 minutes

Cook Time: 10 minutes

Servings: 2

INGREDIENTS

8 oz pre-cooked lump crabmeat

1 egg

1 lemon

1 teaspoon ground crab boil seasoning (Old Bay Seasoning™)

1 tablespoons fresh basil

1 tablespoon fresh parsley

1/4 cup almond meal

1 ripe avocado

Coconut oil (for cooking)

INSTRUCTIONS

1. Heat large skillet over medium-high heat and coat with coconut oil.
2. Slice in half, pit and scoop flesh of half of avocado into medium mixing bowl. Preserve other half.
3. Chop basil and parsley and add to avocado. Zest lemon into bowl to taste. Cut lemon in 1/2 and squeeze about 1 tablespoon of juice into bowl, excluding seeds. Mash well.
4. Add egg to bowl blend. Add crabmeat, crab boil seasoning and almond meal. Mix gently but thoroughly.

5. Form 4 small or 2 large crabmeat patties, pressing firmly to help hold them together. They will be delicate.

6. Add crab patties to hot oiled for about 3 - 4 minutes. Carefully flip and continue cooking for another 3 - 4 minutes on each side, or until golden brown.

7. Drain crab cakes on paper towel. Slice reserved avocado. Plate crab cakes and top with sliced avocado. Serve hot.

Salmon & Veggie Salad

Prep Time: 10 minutes

Cook Time: 10 minutes

Servings: 1

INGREDIENTS

Salad:

1 medium salmon fillet (or 2 oz smoked salmon, do not cook)

1 carrot

1/2 cucumber

8 asparagus stalks

1 cup cabbage

Dressing:

1 avocado

2 tablespoons coconut oil

1/2 lemon

1 small clove garlic

1 tablespoon fresh parsley

1 tablespoon fresh dill

Pinch sea salt

Pinch paprika

INSTRUCTIONS

1. Bring small pot to boil with salted water. Heat small skillet over medium-high heat and lightly coat with coconut oil.

2. Parboil asparagus spears in boiling water for about 2 minutes. Then drain and shock in ice bath.

3. Lay salmon fillet skin-side down in hot oiled skillet. Cook about 3 minutes on each side. Season to taste.

4. Shred or grate cabbage, carrot and cucumber. Drain cucumber in paper towel. Dry asparagus in paper towel and slice into 2 inch pieces. Toss veggies together.

5. Peel garlic and add all *Dressing* ingredients with squeeze of lemon, salt and paprika to taste to food processor or bullet blender. Process until smooth.

6. Plate shredded veggies. Remove salmon fillet and flake off meat over shredded veggies. Or lay smoked salmon slices over veggies.

7. Drizzle salad with avocado *Dressing*. Squeeze a little more lemon juice over salad. Serve immediately.

Pecan Apricot Spinach Salad

Prep Time: 10 minutes

Servings: 1

INGREDIENTS

Salad

2 cups spinach leaves

1/2 cup chopped kale leaves

4 - 5 dried apricots

3 tablespoons pecans (halves or pieces)

Honey Mustard Vinaigrette

2 tablespoons raw honey (or 2 dried dates + 2 tablespoons water)

2 tablespoons ground mustard (or mustard seed)

2 tablespoons raw apple cider vinegar

3 tablespoons raw oil (coconut, walnut, almond, sesame, etc.)

3/4 teaspoons Celtic sea salt

INSTRUCTIONS

1. For *Salad*, rinse, dry and plate spinach and kale. Chop dried apricots. Sprinkle apricots and pecans over greens.
2. For *Honey Mustard Vinaigrette*, add honey, mustard, vinegar, oil and salt to food processor or high-speed blender and process until smooth, about 1 minute.
3. Drizzle *Honey Mustard Vinaigrette* over salad and serve immediately.

Hearty Apple Almond Salad

Prep Time: 5 minutes

Servings: 1

INSTRUCTIONS

1 apple

1 small banana

1/4 cup blueberries

1/4 cup raw almonds

2 dried pitted dates

2 tablespoons pomegranate seeds (or dried goji or noni berries)

1/4 teaspoon ground cinnamon

INGREDIENTS

1. Core and dice apple. Peel and dice banana. Add to serving dish and mix to combine. Top with blueberries.
2. Chop almonds and dates. Or add to food processor and pulse to coarsely grind.
3. Top fruit with chopped nuts and dates. Sprinkle with pomegranate seeds and cinnamon and serve immediately.

Southern Style Egg Salad

Prep Time: 5 minutes

Cook Time: 15 minutes

Servings: 4

INGREDIENTS

8 cage-free eggs

1 avocado

1 celery stalk

1/4 sweet onion

1/4 cup sweet pickle relish (or dill pickle relish + 1 tablespoon raw honey, agave or date butter)

1/4 cup organic mustard

2 teaspoons paprika

1/4 teaspoon Celtic sea salt

INSTRUCTIONS

1. Bring medium pot of lightly salted water to a boil. Leave enough room in pot for eggs.
2. Gently add eggs to hot water with tongs and cook about 10 minutes.
3. Drain eggs into colander in sink. Fill pot with cold water and add eggs back to pot. Let cold water run slowly over eggs in pot to cool.
4. Slice and pit avocado. Scoop flesh into medium mixing bowl. Thinly slice celery. Peel and finely dice onion. Add to mixing bowl

with relish, mustard, salt and spices. Mix with large spoon to combine.

5. Crack cooled eggs and peel off shells. Add boiled eggs to medium mixing bowl.

6. Use a fork or knife to chop eggs. Use large spoon to mix and mash ingredients together until smooth mixture with soft chunks forms. Stir to combine.

7. Transfer to serving dish and serve immediately. Or refrigerate about 20 minutes and serve chilled.

Bunless Portobello Burger

Prep Time: 10 minutes

Cook Time: 35 minutes

Servings: 2

INGREDIENTS

4 large Portobello mushroom caps

12 oz grass-fed ground beef (or chicken, turkey, bison, elk, etc.)

1/2 white onion

Celtic sea salt, to taste

Coconut oil (for cooking)

Portobello Cheese Sauce

4 Portobello stems

3/4 cup cashews

2 tablespoons nutritional yeast

1/2 lemon

1/4 teaspoon mustard powder

1/4 teaspoon Celtic sea salt

Water

Coconut oil (for cooking)

INSTRUCTIONS

1. *Soak cashews in enough water to cover for at least 4 hours, or overnight in refrigerator. Drain and rinse.

2. Preheat oven to 450 degrees F. Heat small pan over medium heat. Add 1 tablespoon bacon fat or coconut oil to hot pan. Line sheet pan with aluminum foil. Place metal cooling or baking rack over lined sheet pan.

3. Remove stems from Portobello mushroom caps. Chop and reserve stems. Place mushroom caps gill-side up on prepared sheet pan. Drizzle caps lightly with coconut oil.

4. Peel onion and slice crosswise into 2 full 1/4 inch cross sections. Keep rings intact and place on prepared sheet pan. Drizzle slightly with coconut oil and sprinkle with salt.

5. Form ground beef into 3/4 inch patties. Place on prepared sheet pan and sprinkle with salt.

6. Bake about 12 minutes, for medium-well burgers. Remove from oven and sprinkle mushroom caps with salt.

7. For *Portobello Cheese Sauce*, add chopped mushrooms stems to hot oiled pan. Sauté until soft and lightly caramelized, about 5 minutes. Stir occasionally.

8. Juice lemon into food processor or high-speed blender. Add cashews, nutritional yeast, salt and spices to processor. Process until smooth, about 2 minutes. Add enough water to reach desired consistency.

9. Add mixture to sautéed mushrooms and stir to heat *Portobello Cheese Sauce* through, about 2 minutes. Remove from heat.

10. Transfer 2 mushroom caps to serving dish, gill-side up. Top with roasted onion ring slice, then hamburger patty. Spoon *Portobello Cheese Sauce* over patty and top with remaining Portobello caps, gill-side down.

11. Serve hot.

Simple Sausage and Peppers

Prep Time: 5 minutes

Cook Time: 20 minutes

Servings: 4

INGREDIENTS

4 large mild Italian sausage links (pork, chicken or turkey)

1 yellow onion

1 green bell pepper

Cracked black pepper, to taste

INSTRUCTIONS

1. Heat large cast iron pan or skillet over medium heat.
2. Add sausage links to hot pan and sear on one side about 8 - 10 minutes.
3. Peel onion. Remove stems, seeds and veins from bell pepper. Chop or slice onion and pepper and add to pan.
4. Turn over sausage links and stir veggies. Sear sausage and sauté veggies until sausage is cooked through and veggies are tender and caramelized, about 8 - 10 minutes. Stir veggies around sausage occasionally. Try not to disturb sausage too much.
5. Transfer sausage to cutting board and slice into 1 1/2 inch pieces, if desired.
6. Transfer *Sausage and Peppers* to serving dish and serve hot.

Lettuce Nut Salad

Prep time: 10 min

Cook time: 6-8 minutes

Serves: 4

INGREDIENTS

1 7oz bag of Romaine lettuce

1 cup strawberries

1 cup blueberries

1 cup kiwi

½ cup almonds

½ cup walnuts

2 cups coconut milk

1 tbsp arrowroot

1 tsp cinnamon

INSTRUCTIONS

1. Dice the fruits. In a saucepan, combine coconut milk, arrowroot, and cinnamon over medium heat. Cook, stirring, for 4 minutes. Add the walnuts and almonds to the sauce and continue cooking until slightly thick.

2. Combine lettuce and fruit in a bowl and drizzle the sauce over the top. Serve immediately or chill 20 minutes and then serve.

Olive Tapenade

Prep Time: 15 minutes

Servings: 2

INGREDIENTS

1 1/2 cups any combination pitted olives (Kalamata, Spanish, black, sweet pimento, etc.)

2 tablespoons capers

2 anchovy fillets

1 garlic clove

2 fresh basil leaves

Squeeze of lemon (optional)

2 tablespoons coconut oil

INSTRUCTIONS

1. Peel garlic and add to food processor or high-speed blender. Process until finely ground.
2. Rinse and drain olives, capers and anchovy fillets. Add to processor with basil, oil and squeeze of lemon. Process until finely chopped or coarsely ground, about 1 - 2 minutes.
3. Transfer to serving dish and serve immediately.

Creamy "Cheesy" Broccoli Soup

Prep Time: 10 minutes

Cook Time: 30 minutes

Servings: 4

INGREDIENTS

1 large head broccoli

2 cups vegetable broth

1 cup nut milk

1/2 cup nutritional yeast

1 medium onion (white or yellow)

2 garlic cloves

1 tablespoon coconut aminos (or liquid aminos or tamari)

1 tablespoon mustard powder

Celtic sea salt, to taste.

2 tablespoons bacon fat (or coconut oil, cacao butterr ghee)

Water

INSTRUCTIONS

1. Heat medium pot over medium heat. Add fat or oil to hot pot.

2. Peel onion and garlic. Chop and add to hot pot. Sauté until fragrant, about 2 minutes.

3. Chop broccoli and add to pot with vegetable broth. Increase heat and bring to boil. Cover and boil about 15 - 20 minutes until broccoli is softened.

4. Pour pot in to food processor or high-speed blender with nutritional yeast, coconut aminos, spices and salt, to taste. Process until smooth, about 1 - 2 minutes. Add enough water to reach desired consistency.

5. Transfer to serving dish and serve immediately. Or add back to pot and heat through over medium heat. Then serve.

Kelp Noodle Stir-Fry

Prep Time: 10 minutes

Cook Time: 10 minutes

Servings: 2

INSTRUCTIONS

1 (12 oz) package kelp noodles

8 oz grass-fed beef

1/2 sweet onion

1 red bell pepper

2 cloves garlic

1 inch piece fresh ginger

1/2 teaspoon paprika

1/4 teaspoon sea salt

Small bunch fresh cilantro

Squeeze of lime (optional)

Coconut oil (for cooking)

DIRECTIONS

1. Heat large skillet or medium cast-iron wok over high heat. Drain and rinse kelp noodles. Add to medium bowl and soak for 5 minutes in water and juice of 1/2 lime.
2. Stem and seed peppers. Peel onion, garlic and ginger. Dice beef into strips and add to medium mixing bowl. Mince garlic and ginger. Add to beef with salt, paprika and 1 teaspoon coconut oil. Mix with wooden spoon to evenly coat beef.

3. Slice onion and bell pepper and add to hot skillet. Sauté about 2 minutes. Add seasoned beef to skillet and sauté another 2 minutes to brown.

4. Drain kelp noodles and add to skillet. Stir until beef is browned and cooked to about medium-well, kelp noodles are heated through, and veggies caramelize.

5. Remove skillet from heat and plate stir-fry. Chop fresh cilantro.

6. Top stir-fry with cilantro and squeeze of lime if desired.

7. Serve hot.

Veggie Burger

Prep Time: 5 minutes

Cook Time: 20 minutes

Servings: 4

INGREDIENTS

Soft Burger Bun

Veggie Burger

2 eggs

1/2 head cauliflower

2 medium carrots

1 small white onion

1 cup walnuts (1/2 cup ground)

1/4 cup almond flour

2 tablespoons tapioca flour

2 tablespoons ground chia seed (or flax meal)

2 cloves garlic

1 teaspoon paprika

1 teaspoon sea salt

Topping

1 avocado

1 onion

2 ribs romaine lettuce (or preferred lettuce)

INSTRUCTIONS

1. Preheat oven to 350 degrees F. Line sheet pan with parchment paper, or lightly coat with coconut oil. Or lightly coat 6 mini round cake pans with coconut oil.

2. Prepare *Soft Burger Buns* and place in oven.

3. While bread bakes, line dish with parchment paper.

4. Add walnuts and almond four to food processor or bullet blender. Process until finely ground. Add to medium mixing bowl.

5. Peel small onion and garlic. Add to processor or blender with cauliflower and carrots. Process until finely ground. Add eggs, tapioca and chia. Process until mixture becomes thickened and has batter-like consistency.

6. Add veggie mixture and spices to mixing bowl. Mix all ingredients together with hands or wooden spoon until fully combined and uniform.

7. Form veggie mixture into 4 patties and place on parchment lined dish. Place in freezer for 10 minutes.

8. Heat medium skillet over medium-high heat and add 1 tablespoon coconut oil.

9. Peel onion. Make 4 thick slices, keeping full ring intact. Using spatula, place full rings into hot oiled pan. Sear 1 minute on each side. Set aside on paper towel to drain.

10. Reduce heat to medium and coat pan with coconut oil.

11. Remove veggie patties from freezer and place in hot oiled pan. Cook 5 minutes, then carefully flip with spatula and cook another 5 minutes.

12. Remove *Soft Burger Bun* from oven and let cool about 5 minutes.

13. Cut lettuce ribs in half. Slice avocado in half, pit and slice flesh in peel.
14. Slice bun in half and place lettuce on bottom bun. Add burger patty, then grilled onion ring. Finish with a few slices of avocado and top bun.
15. Serve immediately.

Crispy Fish Sandwich with Quick Slaw

Prep Time: 20 minutes

Cook Time: 20 minutes

Servings: 1

INGREDIENTS
Soft Burger Bun

Crispy Fish

6 oz fillet white fish (cod, tilapia, catfish, etc.)

1/4 cup almond meal

1 egg

1/2 teaspoon sea salt

Quick Slaw

1/4 head cabbage (1 cup shredded)

1 small carrot

2 tablespoons coconut oil

1 - 2 tablespoons apple cider vinegar

1 tablespoon sweetener* (optional)

1 teaspoon sea salt

DIRECTIONS

1. Preheat oven to 350 degrees F. Line sheet pan with parchment paper, or lightly coat with coconut oil. Or lightly coat 6 mini round cake pans with coconut oil.

2. Prepare *Soft Burger Buns* and place in oven.

3. While bread bakes, heat small skillet over medium heat and coat with coconut oil.

4. For *Quick Slaw*, remove any tough outer leaves and core from cabbage. Shred cabbage and carrot. Add to medium mixing bowl with vinegar, coconut oil, sweetener, salt and pepper. Toss to combine and place in refrigerator.

5. For *Crispy Fish*, beat egg with half of salt in small mixing bowl. Mix almond flour with remaining salt in small dish.

6. Coat fish fillet in egg then dredge in almond flour. Place fillet in hot oiled pan and cook about 3 minutes on each side, until crispy and golden but still juicy.

7. Remove fish from pan and drain on paper towels.

8. Remove *Soft Burger Bun* from oven and let cool about 5 minutes.

9. Slice bun in half and add *Crispy Fish*. Top with *Quick Slaw* and serve immediately.

stevia, raw honey or agave nectar

Grain-Free Soft Burger Buns

Prep Time: 5 minutes

Cook Time: 15 minutes

Servings: 6

INGREDIENTS

1/4 cup almond flour

1/4 cup coconut flour

4 eggs

2 tablespoons coconut oil

2 tablespoons unsweetened applesauce

1 teaspoon flax meal (or ground chia seed)

1 teaspoon baking powder

1/2 teaspoon sea salt

INSTRUCTIONS

1. Preheat oven to 350 degrees F. Line sheet pan with parchment paper, or lightly coat with coconut oil. Or lightly coat 6 mini round cake pans with coconut oil.

2. Beat eggs, coconut oil and applesauce in medium mixing bowl with hand mixer or whisk.

3. In large mixing bowl, sift together coconut flour, almond flour, flax or chia meal, baking powder and salt. Pour egg mixture into flour mixture and mix until combined.

4. Scoop thick batter onto prepared sheet pan in six 4 inch rounds. Or pour into six prepared mini cake pans for uniformity. Smooth batter with knife or spatula.

5. Place in oven and bake for 12 - 15 minutes, or until tops are firm to the touch and golden.

6. Remove from oven and let cool at least 5 minutes.

7. Slice in half and serve with your favorite patty or filling.

Chicken Tenders

Prep Time: 5 minutes

Cook Time: 10 minutes

Servings: 2

INGREDIENTS

8 oz boneless, skinless chicken

1 egg

1/2 cup almond meal

1 teaspoon flax meal

1 teaspoon paprika

1/2 teaspoon thyme

1/2 teaspoon onion powder

1/2 teaspoon sea salt

Honey Mustard

2 tablespoon raw honey or agave nectar

3 tablespoons organic mustard

INSTRUCTIONS

1. Heat a medium skillet over medium high heat. Lightly coat pan
    with coconut oil.
2. Slice chicken into 1 inch wide strips. Arrange slices between 2
    sheets of parchment and pound with kitchen mallet or rolling pin to
    flatten slightly. Place flattened pieces between two paper towels to
    absorb excess moisture.

3. In a shallow dish, blend almond meal, flax meal, spices and salt.

4. Beat egg in small mixing bowl. Dip chicken into beaten egg, then dredge in seasoned almond meal.

5. Carefully place coated chicken strips into hot oil and fry about 3 - 4minutes, until golden brown and cooked through. Turn with tongs half way through cooking.

6. Drain cooked chicken on paper towel, then transfer to serving dish. Serve warm.

7. Or allow to cool and transfer to lidded container. Serve room temperature or chilled.

8. Mix mustard and sweetener in small serving bowl or lidded container. Serve with chicken.

*stevia, raw honey or agave nectar

Soft Baked Pretzel

Prep Time: 15 minutes

Cook Time: 20 minutes

Servings: 4

INGREDIENTS

1 cup coconut flour

1/2 cup tapioca flour/starch

1/2 cup coconut oil

1/2 cup water

1 egg

2 tablespoon apple cider vinegar

1/2 teaspoon baking soda

1/2 teaspoon baking powder

1/2 teaspoon sea salt

INSTRUCTIONS

1. Preheat oven to 350 degrees F. Heat medium pan over medium-high heat. Line sheet pan with parchment or baking mat.
2. Add coconut oil, water, vinegar and salt to pot. Bring to a boil and remove from heat.
3. Whisk in tapioca flour. Stir with wooden spoon or soft spatula until mixture gels and comes together.
4. Stir in baking soda and baking powder. Continue mixing for a minute. Mixture will foam and expand. Let mixture sit and cool about 5 minutes.

5. Sift in coconut flour. Mix partially, then beat in egg. Blend until combined. Excess coconut flour may sit in bottom of bowl.

6. Turn out dough onto cutting board dusted with any excess coconut flour from mixture. Knead dough for 2 minutes.

7. Cut dough into 4 equal portions. Roll out pieces into ropes and twist to form classic pretzel twist. Pinch together any crumbled dough.

8. Arrange pretzels on lined sheet pan. Brush with coconut oil or full-fat coconut milk and sprinkle with salt.

9. Place sheet pan in oven and bake about 25 minutes, until cooked through.

10. Serve immediately with organic mustard. Or allow to cool and serve room temperature.

Sausage Stuffed "Corn" Muffin

Prep Time: 10 minutes

Cook Time: 20 minutes

Servings: 12

INGREDIENTS

1 cup almond flour

2 eggs

1/4 cup coconut oil

2 tablespoons unsweetened applesauce

1 teaspoon sweetener*

1 teaspoon apple cider vinegar

1 teaspoon baking powder

1/2 teaspoon ground turmeric

Filling

8 oz ground natural lean sausage (or sausage patties)

2 teaspoons ground sage

INSTRUCTIONS

1. Preheat oven to 350 degrees F. Line muffin pan with paper liners or lightly coat with coconut oil. Heat small skillet over medium-high heat.

2. Add sausage and sage to skillet and sauté about 5 - 8 minutes, until cooked through. Break up sausage if in patties.

3. Beat eggs in medium mixing bowl with hand mixer or whisk until thick and slightly foamy. Add oil, applesauce, sweetener and vinegar. Mix well.

4. Stir in almond meal, baking powder and turmeric until combined.

5. Use ice cream scoop or tablespoon to scoop batter into muffin tins, about 1/4 - 1/3 full. Spoon sausage over batter. Then top with second scoop of batter. Fill each muffin cup only 1/2 - 2/3 full.

6. Bake 15 - 18 minutes until edges are golden brown and tops are firm.

7. Serve warm. Or allow to cool and serve room temperature.

*stevia, raw honey or agave nectar

Chicken and Waffles

Prep Time: 20 minutes

Cook Time: 15 minutes

Servings: 2

INGREDIENTS

Waffles

1 cup almond flour

1/4 coconut flour

3 cage-free eggs (separated)

1/4 cup coconut oil (or coconut or cacao butter, melted)

1/4 cup raw honey (or agave, date butter or stevia)

2 teaspoons aluminum-free baking soda

1 teaspoon vanilla

Pinch Celtic sea salt

Coconut oil (for cooking)

Raw honey, agave, fruit syrup (for garnish, optional)

Chicken Strips

8 oz (1/2 lb) boneless, skinless chicken (white or dark meat)

1 cage-free egg

1/2 cup coarse almond meal (or almond flour)

1 teaspoon flax meal

1/2 teaspoon paprika

1/2 teaspoon Celtic sea salt

INSTRUCTIONS

1. Preheat waffle iron. Use wadded paper towel to carefully coat cooking surface with coconut oil. Heat medium pan over medium-high heat. Lightly coat pan with coconut oil.

2. For *Waffles*, in medium mixing bowl, beat egg whites to medium-stiff peaks with hand mixer, about 5 minutes.

3. In small mixing bowl, combine flours, salt and baking soda. In large mixing bowl, beat together egg yolks, oil or butter, sweetener and vanilla with hand mixer or whisk.

4. Beat flour mixture into egg yolk mixture. Gently fold egg whites into egg yolk batter.

5. Pour portion of batter onto hot waffle iron. Do not overfill. Cook 4 - 5 minutes, until golden brown and crisp. Repeat with remaining batter. Set aside cooked *Waffles*.

6. For *Chicken Strips*, cut chicken into equal portions. Add almond meal, flax meal, salt and spices to shallow dish and blend.

7. Add egg to separate shallow dish and beat. Dip and coat chicken in beaten egg, then dredge and coat well in almond meal mixture.

8. Carefully place coated chicken in hot oiled pan. Cook until golden brown and cooked through, about 3 - 4 minutes per side, depending on thickness. Turn with tongs halfway through cooking.

9. Remove *Chicken Strips* from pan and place on paper towel to drain.

10. Transfer cooked *Waffles* to serving dish. Top with *Chicken Strips*. Drizzle with raw honey, agave, or your favorite fruit syrup (optional).
11. Serve immediately.

Sweet Potatoes Roast

Prep time: 10 minutes

Cook time: 30 minutes

INGREDIENTS

3 sweet potatoes

¼ cup extra virgin olive oil

¼ tsp Celtic sea salt

¼ tsp smoked paprika

INSTRUCTIONS

1. Preheat oven to 500 degrees.
2. Peel the potatoes and cut them into small wedges. In a large bowl, combine potato wedges, extra virgin olive oil, Celtic sea salt and smoked paprika. Mix well until all wedges are coated in all ingredients.
3. Place on a baking sheet and bake for 30 minutes, turning once halfway through, and continue cooking until they are well browned.
4. Remove from oven and let cool. Serve.

Red Pepper Crab Soup

Prep Time: 20 minutes

Cook Time: 1 hour 20 minutes

Servings: 4

INGREDIENTS

12 oz (3/4 lb) cooked crabmeat (flaked or chopped lump)

4 red bell peppers

4 cups chicken broth (or seafood stock)

1 parsnips

1 cup lite coconut milk

1 cup full-fat coconut milk

1/2 teaspoon garlic powder

1/2 teaspoon dried basil

1 teaspoon Celtic sea salt

INSTRUCTIONS
1. Set oven to BROIL.
2. Remove stems, seeds and veins from bell peppers. Roughly chop and lay skin side up on sheet pan. Broil until skin blackens, about 5 - 10 minutes.
3. Transfer to lidded container and let steam for 10 minutes. Remove skins and discard.
4. Chop parsnips. Add roasted, skinned peppers to medium pot with broth or stock and parsnips. Bring to a boil over high heat.

5. Add coconut milk, salt and spices. Reduce heat to medium and simmer for 45 minutes. Stir occasionally.

6. Add to food processor or high-speed blender in batches and process until puréed. Or purée in pot with immersion blender.

7. Add puréed mixture back to pot and heat over medium heat. Stir in crab meat and warm through, about 5 minutes.

8. Transfer to serving dish and serve hot.

Chicken and "Rice"

Prep Time: 10 minutes

Cook Time: 30 minutes

Servings: 4

INGREDIENTS

16 oz (1 lb) skin-on bone-in chicken

1/3 head cauliflower

4 cups chicken broth (or stock)

2 large carrots

2 large celery stalks

2 teaspoons dried thyme

3 bay leaves

1 teaspoon ground black pepper (or white pepper)

Celtic sea salt, to taste

INSTRUCTIONS

1. Heat medium pot over medium-high heat. Place chicken skin-side down in hot pot. Sear and render out fat for about 5 minutes. Turn and brown on flesh side about 5 minutes.
2. Add cauliflower to food processor with shredding attachment and process to "rice." Or mince. Set aside. Dice carrots and celery.
3. Remove chicken from hot pot and set aside. Add veggies to pot and sauté about 5 minutes.

4. Add chicken back to pot with chicken stock, spices and salt, to taste. Increase heat to high and bring to simmer. Let simmer about 15 minutes, until veggies are tender and chicken is cooked through.
5. Transfer to serving dish and serve immediately.

Dinner

Coconut Chicken Bites

Prep Time: 10 minutes

Cook Time: 15 minutes

Servings: 4

INGREDIENTS

16 oz (1 lb) boneless, skinless chicken

3 cage-free egg whites

1 cup flaked or shredded coconut

1/4 teaspoon ground ginger

1/2 teaspoon garlic powder

1 teaspoon Celtic sea salt

Coconut oil (for cooking)

Coconut Glaze

1/3 cup raw honey (or agave)

1/3 cup coconut milk

1/4 cup flaked or shredded coconut

1 tablespoon fresh lime juice

1/4 teaspoon ground ginger

Pinch Celtic sea salt

Water

INSTRUCTIONS

1. Preheat oven to 425 degrees F. Line sheet pan with parchment paper. Or place oven-safe wire rack over sheet pan.

2. Add coconut to shallow dish. Set aside.

3. Add egg whites, ginger, garlic and salt to large mixing bowl. Beat with hand mixer or whisk until light and fluffy, about 2 - 4 minutes.

4. Cut chicken into 1 inch cubes and add to egg whites. Toss to coat.

5. Let excess egg white drain from chicken, then add to coconut flakes. Toss to coat. Return chicken to egg whites, then coconut flakes again. Press chicken into flaked coconut and coat well.

6. Place coated chicken on prepared sheet pan. Brush lightly with coconut oil.

7. Place in oven and bake for about 5 minutes. Turn chicken over and brush with coconut oil. Bake about 5 minutes, until coconut is golden brown and chicken is cooked through are bright pink.

8. For *Coconut Sauce*, add honey, coconut milk, shredded coconut, lime juice, ginger and salt to small pot. Add water to reach desired glaze consistency, if necessary.

9. Heat over medium heat and bring to simmer. Remove from heat and transfer to large mixing bowl.

10. Remove chicken from oven and add to bowl. Toss with *Coconut Sauce*.

11. Transfer to serving dish and serve hot.

Cashew Chicken

Prep Time: 5 minutes

Cook Time: 10 minutes

Servings: 2

INGREDIENTS

12 oz (3/4 lb) boneless skinless chicken

1/2 cup raw cashews

1/2 small onion (white or yellow)

1/2 red bell pepper

1/2 green bell pepper

1 small celery stalk

2 tablespoons tamari (or coconut aminos or apple cider vinegar)

1 teaspoon raw honey (or agave or date butter)

1 garlic clove

1/2 inch piece fresh ginger

1/2 teaspoon Celtic sea salt

Bacon fat or coconut oil (for cooking)

INSTRUCTIONS

1. Heat large pan or wok over medium heat. Lightly coat with bacon fat or coconut oil.

2. Peel and mince garlic and ginger. Remove seeds, stems and veins from peppers, then roughly chop. Dice carrot. Slice celery.

3. Roughly chop chicken and season with salt.

4. Add garlic and ginger to hot oiled pan or wok. Sauté about 1 minute, until fragrant. Add seasoned chicken add sauté until browned, about 2 minutes. Transfer chicken to small bowl and set aside.

5. Add veggies to hot oiled pan. Sauté until tender and lightly browned, about 2 minutes. Add tamari, honey and cashews. Sauté until veggies are just cooked, but still crisp.

6. Add chicken back to pan and heat until just cooked through, about 2 minutes.

7. Transfer to serving dish and serve hot.

Korean Beef

Prep Time: 5 minutes*

Cook Time: 20 minutes

Servings: 4

INGREDIENTS

16 oz (1 lb) beef sirloin

1 medium carrot

1 green onion (scallion)

1/2 onion (yellow or white)

3 tablespoons tamari (or coconut aminos or liquid aminos)

1 tablespoon sesame oil

1 tablespoon sesame seeds

1 teaspoon raw honey (or agave)

1 garlic clove

1/2 teaspoon Celtic sea salt

INSTRUCTIONS

1. Peel and mince garlic. Add to large kitchen bag or medium container with lid with tamari, sesame oil, sesame seeds, honey and salt. Mix to combine.

2. Peel and chop onions. Julienne (thinly slice lengthwise) carrots. Chop green onion. Thinly slice beef. Add to container and toss or mix well to coat. Set aside in refrigerate at least 3 hours to marinate.

3. Heat outdoor grill to high heat.

4. Drain beef and vegetables from marinade and place on large sheet of aluminum foil. Fold foil over meat and veggies to make sealed packet.
5. Place on grill and cook 20 minutes, for about medium-well doneness.
6. Carefully remove packet from grill and place on cutting board. Carefully open one end of packet and release steam for about 1 minute. Open packet and transfer meat and veggies to serving dish.
7. Serve hot.

Chicken and Dumplings

Prep Time: 10 minutes

Cook Time: 40 minutes

Servings: 4

INGREDIENTS

Chicken Soup

16 oz (1 lb) skin-on bone-in chicken pieces

3 cups organic chicken broth or stock

3 cups water

2 carrots

2 celery stalks

1/2 small white onion

2 bay leaves

2 teaspoons dried thyme (or 4 teaspoons fresh thyme)

1/2 teaspoon paprika

1 teaspoon Celtic sea salt

Dumplings

1 1/2 cups almond flour

1/4 cup arrowroot powder

1 cage-free egg

1/4 cup chilled coconut oil (or room temperature coconut or cacao butter)

1/2 teaspoon baking soda

1/2 ground bay leaf

1/2 teaspoon garlic powder

1/2 teaspoon Celtic sea salt

Nut milk or chicken broth or stock

INSTRUCTIONS

1. Heat large pot over medium-high heat. Place chicken skin-side down in hot pot. Sear and render out fat for about 5 minutes.

2. Chop carrots and celery. Peel onion and mince. Add veggies to chicken with salt.

3. Turn chicken over and brown on flesh side about 5 minutes. Stir veggies occasionally.

4. Add bay, thyme and paprika, chicken stock and water to pot. Increase heat to high and bring to a boil. Reduce heat and simmer about 25 minutes. Place lid loosely over pot to prevent splatter, if necessary.

5. For *Dumplings*, sift almond flour and arrowroot into medium mixing bowl. Cut in solid oil or butter with fork until crumbly mixture forms. Add egg, salt and spices, baking soda, and enough nut milk or chicken broth to bring together soft, slightly sticky dough.

6. Use tablespoon or small scoop to gently drop dough into *Chicken Soup*. Cover with well-fitting lid and let simmer about 10 minutes.

7. Gently stir soup to prevent *Dumplings* from sticking. Turn over any *Dumplings* that are not submerged. Continue simmering 5 minutes, or until *Dumplings* are cooked through.

8. Remove from heat and transfer to serving dish. Use large serving spoon or ladle to serve hot.

Chicken & Berry Salsa

Prep time: 24 hours (date syrup is created overnight)

Cook time: 50 minutes

Servings: 4

INGREDIENTS

Date Syrup

1 cup water

1 cup pitted dates

Salad

4 pieces grass-fed chicken thighs, coarsely chopped

1 tbsp extra virgin olive oil

7 oz bag Romaine lettuce

1 red bell pepper

1 yellow bell pepper

½ cup walnuts

1 cup strawberries

1 cup kiwi

INSTRUCTIONS

1. For Date Syrup, split the dates down the middle, remove the pits, and place in a bowl with 1 cup water. Place this mixture in the fridge overnight. Stir occasionally if you are able to.

2. Preheat oven to 375. Take the chopped chicken thighs and coat them in olive oil. Place them on a baking dish, cover with aluminum foil, and place them in the oven for 30 minutes.

3. Chop the peppers and slice the strawberries and kiwi.

4. When the chicken has cooked for 30 minutes, remove the aluminum foil and cook for another 15 minutes. After 15 minutes, drizzle half the date syrup mixture over the chicken and cook another 5 minutes.

5. Place the romaine lettuce, peppers, walnuts, strawberries and kiwis in a bowl and toss.

6. Remove chicken from oven and place into the bowl. Drizzle the remaining date syrup over the finished dish and toss.

7. Serve immediately or chill 20 minutes and serve.

Roasted Turkey Legs

Prep Time: 10 minutes*

Cook Time: 1 hour 20 minutes

Servings: 4

INGREDIENTS

2 large turkey legs

1/2 teaspoon garlic powder

1/2 teaspoon onion powder

1/2 teaspoon dried rosemary

1/2 teaspoon dried thyme

1/2 paprika (or smoked paprika or Hungarian paprika)

1/2 teaspoon Celtic sea salt

1 1/2 tablespoon coconut oil

Brine

4 cups water

1/4 cup Celtic sea salt

1/4 cup raw honey (or agave or date butter)

INSTRUCTIONS

1. *For *Brine*, add water, salt and sweetener to wide, shallow container. Mix to combine. Add turkey legs and submerge completely in *Brine*. Marinate in refrigerator 12 - 24 hours.
2. Preheat oven to 350 degrees F. Place wire rack over sheet pan.

3. Remove turkey legs from brine. Rub salt, spices and oil over turkey legs, and under skin.

4. Place coated turkey legs on wire rack and bake about 35 - 40 minutes. Carefully turn turkey legs over and bake another 35 - 40 minutes, until skin is crisp and meat is cooked through.

5. Remove from oven and let rest about 2 minutes. Then serve hot.

Herb Crusted Pork Chops with Cinnamon Apples

Prep Time: 10 minutes

Cook Time: 30 minutes

Servings: 4

INGREDIENTS

Pork Chops

4 pork chops (bone-in or boneless)

1/2 cup almond flour

2 tablespoons coconut oil (or cacao butter or ghee)

1 sprig fresh rosemary

1 teaspoon dried thyme

Celtic sea salt, to taste

Coconut oil (for cooking)

Cinnamon Apples

4 tart apples

1/4 cup raw honey (or agave or date butter)

1 tablespoon ground cinnamon

2 tablespoons coconut oil (or cacao butter or ghee)

INSTRUCTIONS

1. Preheat oven to 350 degrees F. Heat large pan over medium heat. Add 2 tablespoons oil, butter or ghee to hot pan.

2. Lightly coat wire rack or slotted broiler pan with coconut oil. Place over sheet pan layered with aluminum foil to catch drippings.

3. For *Pork Chops*, pat pork chops dry and sprinkle with salt. Place on wire rack or broiler pan.

4. Remove rosemary needles from stem and chop. Add to small mixing bowl with almond flour, coconut oil, thyme and salt. Mix to form paste.

5. Press seasoned paste into top of each pork chop with fingers to form a 1/8 inch thick crust.

6. Place pork chops in oven and bake about 20 - 25 minutes.

7. For *Cinnamon Apples*, peel and core apple. Cut apples into thick slices and add to large mixing bowl with sweetener and cinnamon. Mix to combine.

8. Add seasoned apples to hot oiled pan. Sauté about 5 minutes, until aromatic and lightly browned. Reduce heat to medium-low and add 1/2 cup water.

9. Cover pan with lid or aluminum foil and simmer about 20 minutes, or until apples are tender. Stir occasionally.

10. Set oven to BROIL and move pork chops about 6 inches away from the heating element. Broil for about 5 minutes, until topping is browned. Rotate halfway through broiling, if necessary. Do not burn topping.

11. Transfer *Cinnamon Apples* to serving dish. Remove pork chops from oven and place over *Cinnamon Apples*.

12. Serve immediately.

Ground Meat Stuffed Peppers

Prep Time: 10 minutes

Cook Time: 50 minutes

Servings: 4

INGREDIENTS

4 bell peppers

16 oz (1 lb) ground meat (beef, pork, chicken, turkey, etc.)

1/2 head cauliflower (1 cup riced)

1/2 cup roasted red peppers

1/4 cup sundried tomatoes

1/4 cup pecans

1/2 small onion (white, yellow or red)

2 tablespoons coconut oil

2 garlic cloves

Medium bunch fresh herbs (parsley, oregano, thyme, etc.)

1 teaspoon Celtic sea salt

Water

INSTRUCTIONS

1. Preheat oven to 350 degrees F.
2. Cut tops off peppers, then remove stems from tops and seeds and veins from bottoms of peppers. Leave bottoms of peppers hollow but do not pierce. Place in baking dish just large enough to fit peppers snuggly. Set aside.

3. Peel onion and garlic. Roughly chop onions, garlic and cauliflower. Add to food processor or high-speed blender with pecans. Pulse about 15 seconds.

4. Add tops of peppers, roasted red peppers, sundried tomatoes, ground meat, salt and fresh herbs to processor. Process until coarsely ground, about 1 - 2 minutes.

5. Use large spoon to stuff peppers with mixture. Add 1/2 cup water to bottom of baking dish. Cover peppers with aluminum foil.

6. Bake 30 minutes. Carefully remove foil and continue baking uncovered 10 - 20 minutes, until stuffing is golden brown and cooked through .

7. Carefully remove from oven and transfer peppers to serving dish. Serve hot.

Beef Pot Roast

Prep Time: 20 minutes

Cook Time: 6 hours

Servings: 8

INGREDIENTS

5 lb bone-in beef pot roast (or bone-in beef chuck)

2 1/2 cups chicken stock (or broth)

1 1/2 cups button mushrooms (about 1/2 pint)

3 carrots

2 celery stalks

1 onion (white or yellow)

2 garlic cloves

2 1/2 tablespoons tapioca flour (or arrowroot powder)

1 tablespoon organic tomato paste

2 sprigs fresh thyme

1 sprig fresh rosemary

1 - 2 tablespoons Celtic sea salt

1 tablespoon ghee (or cacao butter)

2 tablespoons coconut oil (for cooking)

INSTRUCTIONS

1. Heat large skillet over medium-high heat. Add coconut oil to hot pan.

2. Generously season beef on all sides with salt. Sprinkle 1 tablespoon tapioca or arrowroot over beef and pat to coat. Add to

hot oiled pan and sear on all sides until browned, about 5 minutes per side. Set aside in baking dish to rest.

3. Slice mushrooms. Peel and chop onions. Peel and mince garlic.
4. Add ghee or butter and mushrooms to hot pan. Sauté about 2 minutes.
5. Add onions and sauté until translucent, about 5 minutes. Add garlic and sauté about 1 minute.
6. Stir in remaining 1 1/2 tablespoons tapioca or arrowroot and cook about 1 minute. Stir in tomato paste.
7. Slowly stir in chicken stock and bring to simmer, about 5 minutes. Remove from heat.
8. Roughly chop carrots and celery. Add to bottom of slow cooker. Place rested beef over veggies and pour in any juices from beef. Add rosemary and thyme. Add mushroom mixture over beef.
9. Cover slow cooker with lid. Turn on to high and cook 5 - 6 hours, until beef is fork tender.
10. Turn off slow cooker and carefully remove lid. Skim off any fat from surface and remove bones.
11. Transfer to serving dish and serve hot.

Pork Butt Roast

Prep Time: 45 minutes

Cook Time: 6 hours

Servings: 4

INGREDIENTS

4 lbs bone-in pork shoulder (pork butt)

2 tablespoons tamari (or coconut aminos)

1 sprig fresh rosemary

1 teaspoon ground ginger

1 teaspoon onion powder

1/2 teaspoon garlic powder

1/2 teaspoon ground bay leaf

1 teaspoon mustard powder

1 tablespoon Celtic sea salt

INSTRUCTIONS

1. Place pork in slow cooker. Rub in tamari. Remove rosemary needles form stem. Sprinkle herbs, spices and salt over pork, then rub in thoroughly.
2. Cover slow cooker with lid. Turn on to low and cook 8 hours. Reduce temperature to warm and cook 4 - 5 hours, until tender and internal temperature reaches at least 190 degrees F.
3. Turn off slow cooker and carefully remove lid. Remove pork and let rest about 5 minutes. Slice or pull meat from bone.
4. Transfer to serving dish and pour juices over dish. Serve hot.

Garlic and White Wine Steamed Mussels

Prep Time: 10 minutes

Cook Time: 5 minutes

Servings: 6

INGREDIENTS

24 fresh green lipped mussels

3 large garlic cloves

1/4 cup ghee (or coconut oil)

1/2 cup white wine (or sparkling apple cider)

1/2 teaspoon sea salt

Medium bunch fresh parsley

INSTRUCTIONS

1. Have fishmonger clean mussels, or scrub mussels and remove the beards with pliers, if necessary.
2. Heat large pan over medium heat. Add ghee or coconut oil and salt.
3. Peel and mince garlic. Add to hot oiled pan and sauté garlic for a few seconds, until aromatic.
4. Add mussels and wine. Cover and cook 3 - 4 minutes, just until most of the mussels open.
5. Remove pan from heat and discard mussels that do not open. Finely chop fresh parsley and add to pan. Toss to combine.
6. Use tongs or slotted spoon to transfer cooked mussels to somewhat deep serving bowl. Pour cooking liquid over mussels.

7. Serve hot.

Macadamia Crusted Ahi Tuna

Prep Time: 5 minutes

Cook Time: 1 minute

Servings: 1

INGREDIENTS

8 oz ahi tuna fillet

1/4 teaspoon coconut oil

1/4 teaspoon dried thyme

1/4 teaspoon dried tarragon (optional)

1/4 cup whole macadamia nuts (shelled)

1 small garlic clove teaspoon

1 small shallot teaspoon

1/2 teaspoon sea salt

2 tablespoons coconut oil

INSTRUCTIONS

1. Heat medium pan over medium-high heat. Add 2 tablespoons coconut oil to pan.

2. Chop macadamia nuts well. Peel and finely mince garlic and shallot. Set aside.

3. Rub top and bottom of fillet with 1/4 teaspoon coconut oil, salt, thyme and tarragon (optional).

4. Press 1/2 chopped macadamia nuts into each side of fillet.

5. Add garlic and shallots to hot oiled pan and sauté for just a second. Do not burn.

6. Carefully place fish in pan and sear 15 - 30 seconds on each side, for rare to medium rare. Carefully flip half way through cooking.

7. Transfer fillet to serving dish and serve hot with mixed greens or favorite veggies.

Parchment Baked Salmon

Prep Time: 5 minutes

Cook Time: 20 minutes

Servings: 1

INGREDIENTS

8 oz salmon fillet (deboned, skin-on)

6 - 8 medium asparagus stalks

1/2 lemon

1 basil sprig

1 rosemary sprig

1 teaspoon coconut oil

Pinch sea salt

Parchment paper

Kitchen twine

INSTRUCTIONS

1. Place large sheet pan on bottom rack of oven. Preheat oven to 400 degrees F. prepare parchment sheet.

2. Place salmon in middle of parchment sheet skin-side down and sprinkle with salt. Place asparagus stalks next to salmon. Cut lemon into thin slices and place over fish and asparagus. Rub herbs between palms, then lay basil and rosemary sprig over lemon slices. Drizzle 1 teaspoon coconut oil over salmon and asparagus.

3. Gather edges of parchment up over salmon and tie tightly with kitchen twine to form sealed pouch.

4. Place pouch directly on hot baking sheet in hot oven. Bake for 20 minutes.

5. Remove from oven and carefully transfer pouch to serving plate. Carefully open pouch to release steam.

6. Serve hot.

Smoked Salmon Eggs Benedict

Prep Time: 15 minutes

Cook Time: 25 minutes

Servings: 4

INGREDIENTS

4 cage free eggs

6 oz smoked salmon

2 sprigs fresh dill

English Muffins

1/3 cup coconut flour

1/3 cup almond flour

2 eggs

1/4 cup almond milk (or low-fat coconut milk)

2 tablespoons coconut oil

1/2 teaspoon baking soda

1 teaspoon apple cider vinegar

Hollandaise Sauce

1/2 cup ghee or coconut oil (melted)

2 egg yolks

1/2 lemon

1/4 teaspoon sea salt

INSTRUCTIONS

1. Preheat oven to 400 degrees F. Coat 2 mini-round cake pans or 4-inch diameter ceramic ramekins with coconut oil. Bring medium pot to simmer with 1 teaspoon salt and 1 teaspoon apple cider vinegar.

2. For *English Muffins*, mix baking soda and apple cider vinegar In small bowl. Set aside and allow to froth.

3. In medium mixing bowl, beat egg whites with hand mixer or whisk until thick and frothy. Add yolks, almond and coconut flour, nut milk, and coconut oil. Mix gently.

4. Add baking soda and vinegar mixture to bowl and blend well until smooth and free of clumps.

5. Pour batter into pans or ramekins and place on sheet pan. Place in oven and bake 15 -18 minutes, until golden brown and center is firm to the touch.

6. Crack eggs into 4 separate small bowls. Coat or spray metal ladle with coconut oil. Hold ladle over simmering water and pour 1 egg into coated ladle. Slowly tilt edge of ladle into hot water, filling it gently while keeping ladle just submerged in water. Do not let egg float out of ladle or submerge ladle into water entirely. Hold and cook egg about 1 - 2 minutes, until whites are opaque and yolk is warmed but still runny. Place poached egg on paper towel to drain. Repeat with remaining eggs.

7. Remove muffins from oven. Loosen from sides of cake pans or ramekins with knife and turn out onto wire rack to cool.

8. For *Hollandaise Sauce*, add egg yolks, squeeze of lemon, and salt to food processor or high-speed blender. Processor for 30 seconds. While processor or blender is running, drizzle in melted ghee or

coconut oil very slowly. Process until all fat is added and emulsified and sauce thickens a bit, about 2 minutes.

9. Cut slightly cool *English Muffins* in half and transfer to serving dish.

10. Layer *English Muffin* halves with smoked salmon, then top with a poached egg. Pour *Hollandaise Sauce* over poached eggs, to taste. Sprinkle with pinch of salt. Chop dill and sprinkle over eggs.

11. Serve immediately.

Almond Crusted Pan Seared Scallops

Prep Time: 15 minutes

Cook Time:10 minutes

Servings: 2

INGREDIENTS

12 large sea scallops (shelled and cleaned)

1/2 cup organic white wine (or sparkling apple cider)

1/3 cup raw almonds

1 tablespoon ground coriander

1/4 teaspoon fresh ground nutmeg

1/2 teaspoon sea Salt

1/2 tablespoon coconut oil

INSTRUCTIONS

1. Preheat oven to 375 degrees F.
2. Add scallops, wine and 1/4 teaspoon salt to small mixing bowl. Set aside to marinate for 10 minutes.
3. Place almonds on dry baking sheet and place in oven. Toast 7 - 8 minutes.
4. Heat medium pan over medium-high heat and add coconut oil.
5. Remove almonds from oven and add to food processor with coriander, nutmeg, and 1/4 teaspoon salt. Pulse to grind coarsely.
6. Add almond coating to shallow dish. Remove scallops from marinade and coat each side in almond mixture.

7. Place coated scallop in hot oiled pan and grill 2 - 3 minutes on each side.

8. Remove scallops and serve immediately with your favorite greens and vinaigrette.

Crunchy Cashew Chicken

Prep Time: 10 minutes

Cook Time: 15 minutes

Servings: 4

INGREDIENTS

16 oz (1 lb) boneless, skinless chicken

1 cup raw cashews

1/4 cup cashew butter

1 cage-free egg

1/4 teaspoon Chinese 5-spice (optional)

1/4 teaspoon ground ginger

1/4 teaspoon garlic powder

1 teaspoon Celtic sea salt

Bacon fat or coconut oil (for cooking)

Water

INSTRUCTIONS

1. Heat large skillet or pan over medium-high heat. Add 1 - 2 tablespoons bacon fat or coconut oil to hot pan.

2. Add cashews to food processor or high-speed blender. Process until finely chopped or coarsely ground, about 1 minute. Transfer half of cashews to shallow dish.

3. Process remaining cashew until finely ground into flour, about 2 minutes. Transfer cashew flour to separate shallow dish.

4. Add cashew butter and egg to third shallow dish. Mix well to combine. Add enough water to reach saucy consistency.

5. Cut chicken into 1/2 inch strips. Dredge in cashew flour and toss to coat well. Then dip into egg mixture and toss to coat. Place chicken in chopped cashews and press to coat well.

6. Place chicken in hot oiled pan and cook about 1 - 2 minutes on each side, until golden brown and cooked through. Stir occasionally, careful to maintain coating.

7. Transfer cooked chicken to serving dish and serve hot.

Sautéed Mongolian Beef

Prep Time: 15 minutes

Cook Time: 10 minutes

Servings: 2

INGREDIENTS

16 oz (1 lb) beef flank steak

1/4 cup arrowroot powder

2 large green onions

Coconut oil (for cooking)

Sauce

1/3 - 1/2 cup date butter (or raw honey or agave)

1/4 cup pure fish sauce

1/4 cup tamari (or liquid aminos or coconut aminos)

1/4 inch piece ginger

2 garlic cloves

1/2 cup water

Bacon fat or coconut oil (for cooking)

INSTRUCTIONS

1. Add arrowroot to shallow dish. Cut steak against the grain into 1/4 inch pieces. Dip each piece into arrowroot and lightly coat on both sides. Set aside for 10 minutes.

2. Heat large pan or wok over medium heat. Add about 1 cup coconut oil to hot pan.

3. Add coated beef to hot oil and cook for about 3 - 4 minutes, gently can carefully stirring constantly. Use slotted spoon to remove beef from oil and drain on paper towels. Set aside.

4. For *Sauce*, heat medium pan over medium heat. Add 1 tablespoon bacon fat or coconut oil to hot pan.

5. Peel and finely grate ginger and garlic. Add to medium pan and sauté until just golden and aromatic, about 30 seconds. Add fish sauce, tamari, date butter and water. Stir and cook until reduced and thickened, about 2 - 3 minutes.

6. Slice green onions on a diagonal into 1 inch pieces. Add to sauce with beef and sauté about 1 minute.

7. Transfer to serving dish and serve hot.

Grain-Free Chicken and Waffles

Prep Time: 20 minutes

Cook Time: 15 minutes

Servings: 2

INGREDIENTS

Waffles

1 cup almond flour

1/4 coconut flour

3 cage-free eggs (separated)

1/4 cup coconut oil (or coconut or cacao butter, melted)

1/4 cup raw honey (or agave, date butter or stevia)

2 teaspoons aluminum-free baking soda

1 teaspoon vanilla

Pinch Celtic sea salt

Coconut oil (for cooking)

Raw honey, agave, fruit syrup (for garnish, optional)

Chicken Strips

8 oz (1/2 lb) boneless, skinless chicken (white or dark meat)

1 cage-free egg

1/2 cup coarse almond meal (or almond flour)

1 teaspoon flax meal

1/2 teaspoon paprika

1/2 teaspoon Celtic sea salt

INSTRUCTIONS

1. Preheat waffle iron. Use wadded paper towel to carefully coat cooking surface with coconut oil. Heat medium pan over medium-high heat. Lightly coat pan with coconut oil.

2. For *Waffles*, in medium mixing bowl, beat egg whites to medium-stiff peaks with hand mixer, about 5 minutes.

3. In small mixing bowl, combine flours, salt and baking soda. In large mixing bowl, beat together egg yolks, oil or butter, sweetener and vanilla with hand mixer or whisk.

4. Beat flour mixture into egg yolk mixture. Gently fold egg whites into egg yolk batter.

5. Pour portion of batter onto hot waffle iron. Do not overfill. Cook 4 - 5 minutes, until golden brown and crisp. Repeat with remaining batter. Set aside cooked *Waffles*.

1. For *Chicken Strips*, cut chicken into equal portions. Add almond meal, flax meal, salt spices and to shallow dish and blend.

2. Add egg to separate shallow dish and beat. Dip and coat chicken in beaten egg, then dredge and coat well in almond meal mixture.

3. Carefully place coated chicken in hot oiled pan. Cook until golden brown and cooked through, about 3 - 4 minutes per side, depending on thickness. Turn with tongs halfway through cooking.

4. Remove *Chicken Strips* from pan and place on paper towel to drain.

5. Transfer cooked *Waffles* to serving dish. Top with *Chicken Strips*. Drizzle with raw honey, agave, or your favorite fruit syrup (optional).

6. Serve immediately.

Healthy Chicken Pie

Prep Time: 25 minutes*

Cook Time: 45 minutes

Servings: 4

INGREDIENTS

Filling

16oz (1lb) boneless skin-on chicken (or pheasant, game hen, etc.)

2 cups chicken broth

2 large carrots

1 large celery stalk

1 green bell pepper

1 small onion

2 garlic cloves

1/2 lemon

1 cage-free egg

2 tablespoons tapioca flour

2 tablespoons coconut flour

2 teaspoons dried thyme (or 4 teaspoons fresh thyme)

Celtic sea salt (to taste)

Bacon fat or coconut oil (for cooking)

Crust

1 1/2 cup almond flour

1/2 cup coconut flour

3/4 cup cold coconut oil (or room temperature cacao butter)

3 cage-free eggs

2 teaspoons dried thyme

1 teaspoon Celtic sea salt

Water

INSTRUCTIONS

1. *For *Crust*, add almond and coconut flour, thyme and salt to medium mixing bowl. Cut oil or butter into flour with fork until crumbly. Mix in eggs until dough starts to combine together. Mix in enough water to bring together tender dough.

2. *Divide dough in half and roll into round disks. Place one dough round over pie pan or plate and gentle press in. Cover and place in freezer 1 hour. Cover and refrigerate remaining dough.

3. Preheat oven to 350 degrees F. Heat large pot over medium heat.

4. For *Filling*, add 2 tablespoons bacon fat or coconut oil to hot pot. Add chicken pieces skin-side down. Cook chicken until browned and fat renders out, about 5 minutes. Turn chicken over and continue cooking another 5 minutes. Remove chicken from pot and set aside.

5. Add coconut and tapioca flour to pot and whisk until smooth paste forms. Gradually whisk in chicken broth. Simmer about 5 minutes, whisking occasionally.

6. Peel and mince garlic. Peel onion and dice. Remove stems, seeds and veins from bell pepper, then chop. Dice carrots and celery. Add veggies to pot with thyme, salt and lemon juice.

7. Remove skin from par-cooked chicken and chop. Add back to pot.

8. Beat egg in small mixing bowl and slowly spoon in hot chicken stock to temper. Once egg is tempered, add to pot and stir to

incorporate. Simmer for 10 minutes, then remove from heat and set aside.

9. Remove *Crust* from freezer and refrigerator. Carefully ladle *Filling* into bottom frozen *Crust*. Lay top *Crust* over *Filling*. Pinch together and crimp edges of top and bottom *Crust* to seal.

10. Brush top *Crust* with bacon fat or coconut oil and sprinkle with salt. Use knife to cut a few slits in top *Crust*.

11. Bake for 35 - 45 minutes, or until crust is golden. Remove from oven and let to cool at least 15 minutes.

12. Serve warm.

Mirepoix with Red Sauce

Prep time: 7 minutes

Cook time: approx. 15 minutes

Serves: 4

INGREDIENTS

Flounder and Mirepoix

4 flounder fillets

1 tbsp extra virgin olive oil

¼ tsp thyme

¼ tsp parsley

1 clove garlic

1 stalk celery

8 baby-cut carrots

1 small onion

¼ cup water

¼ cup clam juice

Roasted Red Pepper sauce

1 tbsp extra virgin olive oil

1/2 small onion

1 clove garlic

¼ tsp smoked paprika

¼ tsp Celtic sea salt

¼ tsp ground white pepper

2 roasted red peppers

3/4 cup organic chicken stock

1 tbsp arrowroot

INSTRUCTIONS

1. For Mirepoix, finely chop the celery, carrots and 1 onion together and place in a bowl.

2. For Roasted Red Pepper sauce, finely chop the ½ onion and combine all the above listed Roasted Red Pepper sauce ingredients together in a pan. Keep warm over very low heat.

3. Combine thyme, parsley and extra virgin olive oil in a braising pan over medium-high heat. Add mirepoix and cook while stirring for 2-3 min until the vegetables are soft but not browned. Add clam juice and Roasted Red Pepper sauce. Season to taste with Celtic sea salt and ground white pepper. Reduce heat to medium-low and simmer 5 min.

4. Season fillets with Celtic sea salt and ground white pepper. Fold the thin end of each fillet underneath itself and place in the pan. Increase heat to a moderate simmer. Cover and poach 5-7 min until internal temperature reaches 130 degrees.

5. Remove fillets from pan and let rest 2 min. Serve immediately afterward, or chill 20 minutes and then serve.

Nuts & Turkey Burgers

Prep time: 10 minutes

Cook time: 6-12 minutes

Servings: 4

INGREDIENTS

16 oz ground turkey

1 cup walnuts

2 cloves garlic

1 onion

¼ tbsp smoked paprika

INSTRUCTIONS

1. Chop walnuts into smaller pieces, about ⅛" cubes. Mince garlic and chop onion into small pieces, about ¼" pieces.
2. Combine the above with ground turkey and add smoked paprika. Knead it all together and separate into four patties.
3. Cook on the grill on high heat, flipping occasionally, until desired done-ness.

Natural Italian Chicken Sausage

Prep Time: 5 minutes

Cook Time: 10 minutes

Servings: 4

INGREDIENTS

20 oz (1 1/4 lb) chicken (ground meat or whole pieces)

1/2 teaspoon all spice

1 teaspoon fennel seed

1 teaspoon ground sage

1 teaspoon dried thyme

1 teaspoon Celtic sea salt

Natural or synthetic sausage casing (optional)

Piping or kitchen bag (optional)

Coconut oil (for cooking)

INSTRUCTIONS

1. Heat medium skillet over medium heat and lightly coat with coconut oil.
2. Remove chicken skin and bones from pieces and coarsely grind in food processor, high-speed blender or meat grinder, if using.
3. Add ground chicken to medium mixing bowl with salt and spices and mix well.
4. Use meat grinder to stuff mixture into casing. Or scoop mixture into piping bag with no tip or kitchen bag with 1 inch corner

cut off, and pipe into casing. Twist casing tightly in opposite directions to section off 4-inch links while stuffing.

5. Or form into 8 - 12 round patties with hands.

6. Place links or patties in hot oiled skillet. Cook links about 4 - 5 minutes per side, until golden brown and cooked through. Or cook patties about 3 - 4 minutes per side, until golden brown and crisp. Turn halfway through cooking.

7. Drain cooked sausage on paper towel. Serve hot.

Herb Roasted Pork Tenderloin

Prep Time: 10 minutes*

Cook Time: 15 minutes

Servings: 4

INGREDIENTS

1 pork tenderloin

1 teaspoon dried rosemary

1 teaspoon dried thyme

1 teaspoon dried oregano

1 teaspoon dried basil

1 teaspoon dried marjoram (optional)

1 teaspoon Celtic sea salt

Apricot Sauce

1 cup dried apricots

2/3 cup water

1 teaspoon apple cider vinegar (or dry white wine)

INSTRUCTIONS

1. Preheat oven to 425 degrees F. Heat small pan over medium heat.
2. Rub tenderloin with salt and spices, then press into meat so it adheres. Place on sheet pan, or wire rack over sheet pan.
3. Roast for 10 - 15 minutes, until just cooked through and no pink remains. Remove pork from oven and let rest 10 minutes.

4. For *Apricot Sauce*, add dried apricots, water and vinegar to food processor or high-speed blender. Process until smooth, about 1 - 2 minutes.

5. Add *Apricot Sauce* to hot pan and reduce until slightly thickened. Stir well and do not let burn. Remove from heat.

6. Slice pork and transfer to serving dish. Top pork with *Apricot Sauce* and serve warm.

Slow Cooker Herbed Chicken

Prep Time: 10 minutes

Cook Time: 4 hours

Servings: 4

INGREDIENTS

5 lb whole chicken (innards removed)

2 cups chicken stock (or broth)

1/2 cup dry white wine (or 1/4 cup apple cider vinegar + 1/4 cup apple juice)

1 1/2 cups pitted French green olives

2 onions (yellow or white)

1 large celery stalk

1 tablespoon raw honey (or agave)

1 tablespoon organic tomato paste

8 cloves garlic

2 bay leaves

2 sprigs fresh rosemary

1 teaspoon dried thyme

1 teaspoon dried basil

1 teaspoon dried parsley

1 tablespoon dried oregano

1/2 teaspoon ground black pepper

1 teaspoon Celtic sea salt

1 teaspoon dried lavender buds (food grade) (optional)

1 teaspoon dried marjoram (optional)

1 teaspoon fennel seed (optional)

1/2 teaspoon dried tarragon(optional)

1 small bunch flat-leaf Italian parsley (optional)

INSTRUCTIONS

1. Rub tomato paste, honey, salt and spices into chicken, over an under skin where possible.
2. Peel onions. Roughly chop 1 onion and celery, then stuff into chicken cavity. Set aside in slow cooker.
3. Slice remaining onions. Add to slow cooker with chicken stock and white wine.
4. Cover slow cooker with lid. Turn on to high and cook 4 - 5 hours, until meat is cooked through.
5. Turn off slow cooker and carefully remove lid. Carve chicken and transfer to serving dish.
6. Serve hot.

Oysters and Pancetta Gratin

Prep Time: 10 minutes

Cook Time: 5 minutes

Servings: 2

INGREDIENTS

6 live oysters

1 teaspoon coconut oil

2 oz pancetta

1/2 cup almonds

1/4 cup arugula

1/4 cup cherry tomatoes

1 shallot minced

2 tablespoons ghee (or coconut oil)

INSTRUCTIONS

1. Have fishmonger or market personnel shuck and clean oysters.
2. Preheat the oven to 400 F. Add coconut oil medium pan and heat over medium heat. Line sheet pan with parchment or aluminum foil.
3. Thinly slice pancetta and add to pan. Sauté 2 minutes, then remove from pan and set aside.
4. Peel and mince shallot. Chop arugula. Finely chop almonds, or add to food processor or high-speed blender and pulse to roughly grind.

5. Add pat of ghee to each oyster. Then sprinkle minced shallot, chopped arugula and crisped pancetta onto each oyster. Sprinkle with finely chopped or roughly ground almonds.

6. Place oysters on prepared sheet pan and place in oven. Bake 3 - 4 minutes, until top is golden and aromatic.

7. Remove from oven and transfer to serving dish. Slice cherry tomatoes in half and garnish dish.

8. Serve immediately.

Seafood Paella

Prep Time: 10 minutes

Cook Time: 25 minutes

Servings: 4

INGREDIENTS

1 large head cauliflower

8 oz chorizo

8 oz large shrimp

12 live little neck clams

12 live mussels

4 bone-in chicken thighs

1 cup chicken stock (or seafood stock)

1 small white onion

2 tablespoons smoked paprika

1 teaspoon saffron

Pinch sea salt

2 tablespoons coconut oil

INSTRUCTIONS

1. Heat large pan over medium heat and add coconut oil.
2. Peel and chop onion. Add to hot oiled pan and sauté until translucent, about 2 minutes.
3. Add chicken thighs and brown about 5 minutes. Turn chicken over and cook another 5 minutes.

4. Rinse and clean clams and mussels, and remove any beards with pliers. Peel and devein shrimp. Cut chorizo into 1 inch slices. Set aside.

5. Roughly chop cauliflower and add to food processor with shredding attachment, process to "rice." Or mince cauliflower with knife.

6. Add riced or minced cauliflower to chicken and sauté 2 minutes. Add chorizo, clams, mussels and shrimp. Add paprika and saffron and sauté another 2 minutes.

7. Add chicken or seafood stock and stir to combine. Increase heat to high and bring to simmer. Reduce heat to medium-high and cover. Let simmer about 5 - 7 minutes, until liquid evaporates, shrimp is opaque, and mussels and clams open. Discard any that do not open.

8. Plate and serve hot.

Asian Empanada

Prep Time: 20 minutes

Cook Time: 20 minutes

Servings: 4

INSTRUCTIONS

Crust

1 cup almond flour

1 cup coconut flour

2 eggs

3 tablespoons sesame oil (or coconut oil)

1/2 teaspoon garlic powder

1/2 teaspoon onion powder

1/2 teaspoon ground ginger

1/4 teaspoon baking soda

1 teaspoon sea salt

1 tablespoon sesame oil (or coconut oil)

1 tablespoon sesame seeds

Filling

6 oz chicken or shrimp

1/2 head cabbage (1 cup shredded)

1 carrot

1/4 cup mushrooms

2 inch piece fresh ginger

2 garlic cloves

1 tablespoon pure fish sauce

1 teaspoon apple cider vinegar

1 shallot

1 scallion

1 teaspoon sesame oil

DIRECTIONS

1. For *Crust*, sift almond and coconut flour into medium mixing bowl. Add baking soda, spices and salt.

2. Whisk eggs in small mixing bowl, then add to flour and combine. Slowly add 3 tablespoons oil until malleable dough comes together.

3. Roll in plastic wrap or wrap tightly in parchment and refrigerate for 15 minutes.

4. Preheat oven to 400 degrees. Line sheet pan with parchment or baking mat. Cover cutting board with parchment. Het medium pan over medium heat.

5. Shred cabbage, grate carrot, slices mushrooms. Peel and grate ginger. Slice scallion. Peel and mince shallot and garlic. Dice chicken or slice shrimp in half.

6. Add sesame oil to pan. Add chicken or shrimp hot oiled pan with ginger, shallot and garlic. Sauté about 90 seconds. Add cabbage, carrot, and mushrooms and sauté for a minute.

7. Add vinegar and fish sauce. Sauté about 3 minutes until cabbage is wilted. Stir in scallions. Remove from heat and set aside.

8. Remove dough from refrigerator. Divide dough into 4 portions. Roll dough into balls and flatten on parchment covered cutting board with hands. Roll into circles about 1/8 inch thick with rolling pin.

9. Scoop equal portions of *Filling* into center of one side of dough circle. Fold bare half of dough over filled half. Press edges together, letting any trapped air escape. Crimp edges of dough together with fork. Repeat with remaining dough.

10. Bruch tops of empanada with sesame oil and sprinkle with sesame seeds.

11. Arrange empanadas on lined sheet pan and bake 15 - 20 minutes, or until dough is golden and cooked through.

12. Serve immediately. Or allow to cool and store in air-tight container.

Smoked Salmon Avocado Salad

Prep Time: 10 minutes

Servings: 1

INGREDIENTS

Salad

2 cups soft lettuce leaves (looseleaf or butterhead varieties)

1/2 cup watercress or dandelion leaves (optional)

2 oz smoked salmon

1/2 avocado

1 sprig fresh dill

1 tablespoon caviar (optional)

Avocado Cream Dressing

1/2 avocado

1 sprig fresh dill

1 tablespoon lemon juice

1/2 teaspoon ground black pepper

1/2 teaspoon Celtic sea salt

1/2 coconut

Water

INSTRUCTIONS

1. For *Salad*, rinse, dry and plate lettuce and watercress or dandelion leaves (optional). Cut avocado in half and remover pit. Dice or

slice avocado flesh in peel, then scoop onto greens. Lay smoked salmon over greens.

2. For *Avocado Cream Dressing*, remove coconut flesh from peel and add to food processor or high-speed blender with enough water to reach desired consistency. Process until smooth and creamy, about 1 - 2 minutes. Strain mixture through nut milk bag and place back into blender.

3. Scoop remaining avocado flesh into blender. Add lemon juice, 1 sprig dill, salt and pepper and process until well combined and smooth, about 1 minute.

4. Drizzle *Avocado Cream Dressing* over salad. Mince remaining dill and sprinkle over salad. Dollop caviar over salad (optional).

5. Serve immediately.

*stevia, raw honey or dried dates

Sliced Veggies With Chicken

Prep time: 4 minutes

Cook time: 8 minutes

Servings: 4

INGREDIENTS

4 pieces grass-fed chicken thighs

1 onion

2 cloves garlic

3/4 cup sliced carrots

2 handfuls Kale greens

2 tbsp chinese five spice

2 tbsp smoked paprika

1 tbsp olive oil

2 tsp lemon juice

1 tbsp coconut oil

INSTRUCTIONS

1. Mince garlic and chop onion to desired size (medium strips work best). Chop carrots to 1/4" thickness. De-rib the kale and chop it coarsely, wash it and allow water to remain on the leaves. Bring 4 cups of water to a light boil.

2. Heat 1 tbsp olive oil over medium heat in a large pan. Add carrot and onion and cook for 8 minutes, stirring occasionally.

3. Meanwhile, heat 1 tbsp coconut oil over medium heat in a separate pan. Add chicken and cook for 4 minutes. Season chicken with

chinese five spice and smoked paprika and turn, adding more of each spice to the other side of the chicken, cooking for another 4 minutes or until cooked through.

4. Add kale to boiling water and boil until bright green, about 5 minutes. Remove from water and let sit while the vegetables and chicken continue cooking.

5. Add everything into the pan with the vegetables and add 2 tsp lemon juice. Add minced garlic and stir for 1 minute.

6. Serve immediately.

No-Crust Kale Quiche

Prep time: 10 minutes

Cook time: 15 minutes

Serves: 4

INGREDIENTS

8 cage-free eggs

2 tbsp extra virgin olive oil

1 7oz bag of Kale greens

1 shallot

2 cloves garlic

½ lemon

2 tbsp coconut oil

INSTRUCTIONS

1. Place a steamer basket in the bottom of a large pot and fill with water; if you see water rise above the bottom of the basket, pour some out. Bring the water to a boil.
2. Wash the kale and remove the stems. Mince the garlic and shallot and squeeze the juice from the lemon into a bowl.
3. In a large pan, add the eggs and extra virgin olive oil. Scramble the eggs, breaking them up until they form many small pieces, tender yet firm.
4. Place the kale in the pot and steam until tender and bright-green.

5. Remove the kale from the pot and combine with the eggs. Add the garlic, shallot and lemon juice, and drizzle the coconut oil over top. Mix and stir thoroughly.

6. Serve immediately or chill 20 minutes and then serve.

Snacks

Broccoli Fries

Prep time: 15 minutes

Cook time: 20 minutes

INGREDIENTS

1 large bunch of broccoli

2 tbsp extra virgin olive oil

1 tbsp garlic powder

¼ tsp Celtic sea salt

INSTRUCTIONS

1. Preheat oven to 450 degrees. Cut the broccoli into florets.
2. In a large bowl, mix broccoli florets, extra virgin olive oil, garlic powder and Celtic sea salt.
3. Spread the broccoli over a baking sheet and roast for 20 minutes until the edges are crispy.
4. Remove from oven and let cool. Serve.

Nuts & Raisin Bars

Prep time: 5 minutes

INGREDIENTS

1 cup cashews

1 cup raisins

¼ tsp cinnamon

⅓ cup shredded coconut

INSTRUCTIONS

1. In a food processor, combine almonds, raisins and cinnamon, and process into a thick butter.
2. Add the coconut flakes and pulse for 15 seconds.
3. Place the mixture on a piece of wax paper and form it into a square. Place this in the freezer for 20 minutes.
4. Cut the square into appropriately-sized pieces. Serve.

Simple Almond Apricot Balls

Prep Time: 15 minutes

Servings: 12

INGREDIENTS

1/2 cup dried pitted dates

1/3 cup dried apricots

1/3 cup almonds (toasted or roasted, if preferred)

1/4 cup flaked or shredded coconut

1/2 tablespoon raw honey (or agave)

INSTRUCTIONS

1. Add apricots and dates to food processor or high-speed blender. Process until finely chopped, about 1 - 2 minutes.
2. Add almonds and coconut to processor. Process until well ground, about 2 minutes. Add honey and pulse until mixture sticks together, about 30 seconds.
3. Form mixture into 12 balls.
4. Serve immediately. Or store in airtight container in refrigerator up to 2 weeks.

Prosciutto Wrapped Dates

Prep Time: 10 minutes

Cook Time: 15 minutes

Servings: 2

INGREDIENTS

12 dried pitted dates

4 slices nitrate-free prosciutto

2/3 cup unsalted cashew butter

12 wooden toothpicks

Water

INSTRUCTIONS

1. Soak toothpicks in water about 5 minutes.
2. Preheat oven to 375 degrees F. Line sheet pan with parchment or baking mat.
3. Slice dates lengthwise and pry open. Do not separate completely. Stuff opened dates with cashew butter and re-close.
4. Cut prosciutto into thirds lengthwise. Wrap prosciutto around dates and secure with soaked toothpicks.
5. Place secured dates on prepared sheet pan. Bake for about 15 minutes, or until prosciutto is crisp and dates are heated through. Remove and let cool about 2 minutes.
6. Transfer to serving dish and serve warm. Or let cool completely and serve room temperature.

Sweet Cinnamon Pretzel

Prep Time: 10 minutes

Cook Time: 20 minutes

Servings: 4

INGREDIENTS

Cinnamon Pretzel

1 cup coconut flour

1/2 cup tapioca flour/starch

1/2 cup coconut oil

1/2 cup water

2 dried dates

1 egg

2 tablespoon apple cider vinegar

1/2 teaspoon baking soda

1/2 teaspoon baking powder

2 teaspoons ground cinnamon

1/2 teaspoon vanilla

1/2 teaspoon ground ginger

1/2 teaspoon sea salt

Coconut Sweet Cream

1/4 cup full-fat coconut milk

2 tablespoons sweetener

1 tablespoon lemon juice

1/2 teaspoon vanilla

INSTRUCTIONS

1. Preheat oven to 350 degrees F. Heat medium pot over medium-high heat. Line sheet pan with parchment or baking mat.

2. Add dates, coconut oil, water, vinegar and salt to food processor or bullet blender and process until smooth. Pour mixture into pot. Bring to a boil and remove from heat.

3. Whisk in tapioca flour. Stir with wooden spoon or soft spatula until mixture gels and comes together.

4. Stir in baking soda and baking powder. Continue mixing for a minute. Mixture will foam and expand. Let mixture sit and cool about 5 minutes.

5. Sift in coconut flour and spices. Mix partially, then beat in egg. Mix until combined. Excess coconut flour may sit in bottom of bowl.

6. Turn out dough onto cutting board dusted with any excess coconut flour from mixture. Knead dough for 2 minutes.

7. Cut dough into 4 equal portions. Roll out pieces into ropes and twist to form classic pretzel twist. Pinch together any crumbled dough.

8. Arrange pretzels on lined sheet pan. Brush with coconut oil or full-fat coconut milk.

9. Place sheet pan in oven and bake about 25 minutes, until cooked through.

10. For *Coconut Sweet Cream*, mix coconut milk, vanilla, sweetener and lemon juice with had mixer or whisk until thick and creamy. Transfer to serving dish.

11. Serve pretzels immediately with *Coconut Sweet Cream*. Or allow pretzels to cool and refrigerate sweet cream, and serve chilled.

stevia, raw honey or agave nectar

Green Deviled Eggs 'N Ham

Prep Time: 5 minutes

Cook Time: 10 minutes

Servings: 4

INGREDIENTS

8 eggs

1 avocado

1/2 teaspoon salt

2 oz natural ham

2 tablespoons fresh dill

INSTRUCTIONS

1. Bring medium pot of lightly salted water to boil. Gently add eggs to hot water with tongs and cook about 8 - 10 minutes.

2. Drain eggs in colander and cool in cold water.

3. Crack shells and peel eggs. Cut eggs in half lengthwise and scoop out yolks into small bowl. Arrange whites on platter with center hollows facing up.

4. Mash avocado and salt with egg yolks until smooth. Dice ham and dill, separately.

5. Scoop avocado blend into each egg white hollow and sprinkle with ham, then dill.

6. Refrigerate about 20 minutes. Serve chilled.

Baked Sweet Plantains

Prep Time: 5 minutes

Cook Time: 20 minutes

Servings: 1

INGREDIENTS

1 ripe yellow plantain

1 tablespoon sweetener*

2 tablespoons water

1 teaspoon coconut oil

1/2 teaspoon ground cinnamon

INSTRUCTIONS

1. Preheat oven to 400 degrees F. Line baking pan with parchment, or lightly coat with coconut oil.
2. Cut plantain into 3/4 inch slices. Remove peel from each slice.
3. Toss plantains in small bowl with sweetener, water, oil and cinnamon.
4. Arrange plantains in single layer on baking pan. Bake 10 minutes, then turn over and bake another 10 minutes, or until plantains are golden brown and tender.
5. Serve warm.

raw honey or agave nectar

Honey Nut Bun

Prep Time: 15 minutes

Cook Time: 30 minutes

Servings: 4

INGREDIENTS

Bun

1 cup tapioca flour/starch

1/4 - 1/3 cup coconut flour

1 egg

1/2 cup warm water

1/2 cup coconut oil

1 teaspoon apple cider vinegar

1 teaspoon vanilla

1/2 teaspoon cinnamon

1/2 teaspoon baking soda

1/2 teaspoon sea salt

Filling

1 cup walnuts

1/4 cup sweetener*

2 teaspoons cinnamon

1 teaspoon ground ginger

INSTRUCTIONS

1. Preheat oven to 350 degrees F. Line sheet pan with parchment paper or coat with coconut oil. Heat medium skillet over medium-high heat.

2. For *Filling*, mix walnuts, sweetener, cinnamon and ginger in small mixing bowl. Set aside.

3. In medium bowl, sift together tapioca flour, 1/4 cup coconut flour, vanilla, cinnamon, baking soda and salt. Stir in warm water and oil.

4. Whisk egg and vinegar in small bowl. Add egg mixture to flour mixture and mix until well combined.

5. Add 1 tablespoon coconut flour or water at a time if needed to form soft and slightly sticky dough.

6. Divide dough into 4 portions and flatten into round disks. Dust your hand or rolling pin with extra tapioca flour to prevent sticking.

7. Scoop *Filling* into center of dough disks and pinch edges of dough together to create round, sealed ball.

8. Place buns sealed side down on sheet pan and pat down slightly. Bake 20 minutes, or until edges are golden brown and dough is cooked through.

9. Serve immediately. Or store in lidded container.

stevia, raw honey or agave nectar

Coconut Macaroons

Prep Time: 10 minutes

Cook Time: 20 minutes

Servings: 12

INGREDIENTS

6 cage-free egg whites

3 cups flaked coconut

1/2 cup sweetener*

1 tablespoon coconut oil

1 teaspoon vanilla

1/4 teaspoon sea salt

INSTRUCTIONS

1. Preheat oven to 350 degrees F. Line a sheet pan with parchment paper or baking mat.
2. In large mixing bowl, beat room temperature egg whites with hand mixer to stiff peaks, about 7 - 8 minutes.
3. Beat in sweetener, vanilla and salt until combined. Fold in 1 cup of coconut at a time.
4. Use ice cream scoop or spoon to drop rounds of batter onto prepared sheet pan.
5. Bake for about 20 minutes, or until coconut is toasted and browned.
6. Allow to cool on pan for 10 minutes. Then remove from pan.

7. Serve warm. Or allow to cool completely and serve room temperature.

* raw honey or agave nectar

Onion Crumpets

Prep Time: 5 minutes

Cook Time: 15 minutes

Servings: 4

INGREDIENTS

1/3 cup coconut flour

4 eggs

1/4 cup nut milk

2 tablespoons coconut oil

1 tablespoon unsweetened applesauce

1/2 teaspoon baking soda

1 teaspoon organic apple cider vinegar

1 teaspoon onion powder

1/4 teaspoon sea salt

1 teaspoon dehydrated onion flakes (optional)

INSTRUCTIONS

1. Preheat oven to 400 degrees F. Coat 4 mini-round cake pans or 4-inch diameter ramekins with coconut oil.
2. In small mixing bowl, mix baking soda and apple cider vinegar. Set aside and allow to froth.
3. In medium bowl, beat eggs with hand mixer or whisk until thick and lightened. Add flour, nut milk, applesauce, onion powder and salt. Mix to combine.

4. Add baking soda and vinegar mixture to medium bowl. Blend well until smooth.

5. Pour batter into prepared pans or ramekins and sprinkle on dehydrated onion flakes (optional). Bake for 12 - 15 minutes, until slightly golden and center is firm to the touch.

6. Remove muffins from oven. Loosen from sides of pans or ramekins with knife, then turn out.

7. Serve warm. Or let cool complete and serve room temperature.

Apple Bread

Prep Time: 10 minutes

Cook Time: 20 minutes

Servings: 24

INGREDIENTS

2 cups coconut flour

1 cup almond flour

2 tablespoons tapioca flour (or arrowroot powder)

2 eggs

1 tart apple

1 sweet apple

1/2 cup unsweetened applesauce

1/4 cup coconut oil

1/4 cup sweetener*

1 tablespoon baking soda

1 tablespoon apple cider vinegar

1 teaspoon ground cinnamon

1 teaspoon ground ginger

1 teaspoon sea salt

INSTRUCTIONS

1. Preheat oven to 375 degrees F. Line 2 muffin pans with paper liners or coat with coconut oil.
2. Peel, core and grate or dice apples, and place in small bowl. Pour vinegar and spices over apples. Toss to coat.

3. In medium bowl, whisk eggs with hand mixer or whisk until light and thickened, about 2 minutes. Add applesauce, sweetener and coconut oil. Blend until combined. Mix in apples.
4. Sift flours, baking soda and salt into apple mixture and mix until combined.
5. Use ice cream scoop or tablespoon to scoop equal portions of batter into muffin pans until 2/3 - 3/4 full.
6. Place in oven and bake for 15 - 20 minutes, or until golden brown and firm but springy to the touch.
7. Remove form oven and let cool at least 5 minutes.
8. Serve warm/ Or allow to cool completely and serve room temperature.

NOTE: Bake in oiled square baking pan for 35 - 45 minutes or two loaf pans for 45 - 55 minutes for **Apple Bread Loaves**.

*stevia, raw honey or agave nectar

Fruit and Nut Apricot Pockets

Prep Time: 10 minutes

Servings: 4

INGREDIENTS

1 cup dried apricots

1/4 cup cashews

2 - 3 tablespoons dried cranberries

2 - 3 tablespoons dried blueberries

INSTRUCTIONS

1. Roughly chop cashews and add too small mixing bowl with cranberries and blueberries. Mix to combine.
2. Open apricots slightly to reveal pocket. Take pinch of mixed nuts and fruit and stuff apricots. Leave a little room to pinch apricot closed.
3. Transfer to serving dish and serve immediately. Or store in airtight container.

Green Baked Avocado

Prep time: 3 minutes

Cook time: 15-20 minutes

INGREDIENTS

1 avocado

2 cage-free eggs

2 tsp chives

INSTRUCTIONS

1. Preheat oven to 425 degrees.
2. Slice the avocado in half and remove the nut. Scoop out enough flesh from the center of each avocado to contain the contents of 1 egg.
3. Crack the eggs and dump them into the middle of each piece of avocado. Place them on a baking sheet and bake for 15-20 minutes.
4. Remove from oven. Season with chives and serve.

Delicious Apple Smoothie

Prep time: 5 minutes

INGREDIENTS

1 apple (honeycrisp preferred)

4 figs

½ avocado

1 handful kale

1 tsp cinnamon

1 cup apple cider

1. Slice avocado in half and remove the nut. Slice the apple into small pieces. Wash the figs, cut them in half and remove the stems.
2. Combine all ingredients except for the kale into a blender. Blend them until pureed, then add kale and blend until pureed.

Crispy Kale Chips

Prep time: 15 minutes

Cook time: 10-15 minutes

INGREDIENTS

1 handful baby kale greens

¼ tsp garlic powder

2 tbsp coconut oil

¼ tsp Celtic sea salt

INSTRUCTIONS

1. Preheat oven to 350 degrees.
2. In a large bowl, combine 2 tbsp melted coconut oil with kale greens, garlic powder and Celtic sea salt. Mix well.
3. Line a baking sheet with parchment paper and place kale on it. Bake until the edges of the kale are browned, 10-15 minutes.
4. Remove from oven and cool. Serve.

Almond Butter Crunch Granola Bar

Prep Time: 30 minutes

Servings: 8

INGREDIENTS

1 1/2 cup raw almonds

1 cup crunchy almond butter

1/4 cup flax seed (or chia seed)

1/2 cup dried pitted dates

2/3 cup shredded or flaked coconut

1/3 cup raw pumpkin seeds

1/2 teaspoon ground cinnamon

1/2 teaspoon vanilla

1 teaspoon Celtic sea salt

INSTRUCTIONS

1. Line loaf pan with parchment paper.
2. Add flax or chia to food processor or high-speed blender and process until finely ground, about 1 - 2 minutes.
3. Add 1 cup almonds and process until thick, smooth paste forms, up to 5 minutes.
4. Add dates and process until thick, fairly smooth mixture forms about 1 - 2 minutes. Transfer to medium mixing bowl.
5. Add remaining 1/2 cup almonds, almond butter, coconut, pumpkin seeds, cinnamon, vanilla, and salt. Stir to combine with large wooden spoon.

6. Transfer mixture to parchment lined pan and firmly press into bottom with hands or spatula. Place in refrigerator for 20 minutes.

7. Remove from refrigerator and cut into bars.

8. Serve chilled. Or allow to warm to room temperature and serve.

Chicks in a Blanket

Prep Time: 20 minutes

Cook Time: 15 minutes

Servings: 4

INGREDIENTS

1 package (26 count) nitrate/nitrite-free mini turkey links (or chicken links)

3 cage-free egg whites

1/4 cup almond flour

1/4 cup coconut flour

1 tablespoon coconut oil (or cacao butter or ghee) (chilled)

1/2 teaspoon baking powder

1/4 teaspoon garlic powder

1/4 teaspoon onion powder

Celtic sea salt, to taste

Organic mustard (or ketchup) (optional)

INSTRUCTIONS

1. In medium bowl, blend almond flour, coconut flour, baking powder, spices and salt, to taste. Cut chilled oil or butter into flour with fork. Mixture should be crumbly. Refrigerate 15 - 20 minutes.

2. Preheat oven to 400 degrees F. Line sheet pan with parchment or lightly coat with coconut oil.

3. Beat egg whites in medium bowl with whisk or hand mixer until white and frothy, just before soft peaks develop.

4. Remove flour mixture from refrigerator. Gently fold egg whites into flour mixture until just combined.

5. Flatten teaspoon of dough into a rectangle in your fingers. Place link in center of dough and wrap around. Repeat with remaining turkey sausage and dough.

6. Place wrapped links on prepared sheet pan and bake about 15 minutes, until dough is golden brown and links are heated through.

7. Serve hot with mustard or ketchup (optional).

Coconut Crisps

Prep Time: 10 minutes

Cook Time: 10 minutes

Servings: 4

INGREDIENTS

1 cup coconut flour

3/4 cup almond flour

4 egg whites

1/4 cup coconut oil

1/4 cup coconut crème

1/4 cup sweetener

1/2 cup flaked coconut

1 teaspoon vanilla

1/2 teaspoon baking soda

3/4 teaspoon sea salt

INSTRUCTIONS
1. Preheat oven to 375 degrees F. Line sheet pan with parchment paper or coat with coconut oil. Prepare two additional sheets of parchment.
2. Whisk egg and oil with hand mixer or whisk until blended and slightly frothy. Add sweetener, coconut crème and vanilla, and continue blending.
3. Sift in half of flour, baking soda, vanilla and salt. Add coconut flakes. Sift in remaining flour. Stir and bring dough together.

4. Form dough into rectangle and flatten with hands on parchment. Cover with second sheet of parchment and flatten to about 1/4 inch with rolling pin. Remove top layer of parchment.

5. Cut rectangles from dough with pizza cutter or sharp knife. Carefully flip dough onto sheet pan. Arrange at least 1/2 inch apart on sheet pan.

6. Bake for about 10 minutes, or until crisp and golden brown. Remove and let cool. Serve room temperature.

Apple Dump Muffins

Prep Time: 15 minutes

Cook Time: 25 minutes

Servings: 12

INGREDIENTS

6 medium apples

1 cup almond flour

1/4 cup tapioca flour

3 eggs

1/2 cup coconut oil

1/2 cup sweetener*

2 teaspoons baking powder

2 tablespoons ground cinnamon

1 teaspoon ground nutmeg

1 teaspoon sea salt

Juice of lemon half

INSTRUCTIONS

1. Preheat oven to 350 degrees F. Lightly coat muffin pan with coconut oil, or line with paper liners.

2. Peel, core and thinly slice apples. Add to medium bowl with 1 tablespoon cinnamon and juice of half a lemon. Evenly sprinkle on tapioca flour and carefully toss with hands to coat apples.

3. In medium mixing bowl, blend almond flour, baking powder, spices and salt. Beat in eggs, sweetener and coconut oil with hand mixer or whisk. Fold in sliced apples.

4. Scoop batter into muffin pan and bake for 20 -25 minutes, or until top is browned and firm but springy. A toothpick inserted into the center should come our moist but clean.

5. Serve warm solo, or drizzled with your favorite sweetener.

NOTE: For *Apple Dump Cake*, bake in square baking dish or Bundt pan for 40 - 50 minutes.

raw honey, agave nectar or maple syrup

Ants On A Log

Prep Time: 5 minutes

Cook Time: 5 minutes

Servings: 2

INGREDIENTS

3 celery stalks

2 tablespoons raisins

Cashew Butter

1 cup cashews

1 teaspoon coconut oil

1/2 teaspoon ground cinnamon

INSTRUCTIONS

1. Add cashews, cinnamon, and coconut oil to food processor or bullet blender. Process until smooth. Let mixture rest between periods of processing to reach desired consistency, if necessary.

2. Cut celery stakes into thirds and fill wells with *Cashew Butter*. Place raisins on cashew butter.

3. Serve room temperature. Or refrigerate 10 minutes and serve chilled.

Piña Colada Smoothie

Prep Time: 5 minutes

Cook Time: 5 minutes

Servings: 2

INSTRUCTIONS

1 large banana

1 cup pineapple chunks (fresh, frozen or canned)

2 tablespoons flaked coconut

1 cup coconut milk

1 cup ice (crushed preferably)

DIRECTIONS

1. Add banana, pineapple, coconut, coconut milk and ice to highs-speed blender. Process until smooth.

2. Pour into chilled glasses and serve immediately.

Awesome Strawberry Chia Pudding

Prep Time: 10 minutes*

Servings: 2

INGREDIENTS

2 coconuts (or 1 cup flaked coconut)

2 - 4 tablespoons raw honey (or dried pitted dates)

1/4 cup tablespoons whole chia seeds

1 cup strawberries (fresh or frozen and thawed, chopped)

1/2 teaspoon vanilla

Water

INSTRUCTIONS

1. *Soak flaked coconut in 2 cups water overnight in refrigerator, if using. Soak dates in enough water to cover at least 4 hours, or overnight in refrigerator, if using. Drain dates.

2. Add soaked coconut and soaking liquid to high-speed blender. Or remove flesh from fresh coconuts and add to high-speed blender with 2 cups water. Process until well blended and fairly smooth, about 1 - 2 minutes.

3. Strain mixture through nut milk bag, cheesecloth or strainer back into blender.

4. Reserve pulp and set aside to dry and dehydrate, then use as coconut flour.

5. Remove stems from strawberries, then cut in half. Add to blender with honey or dates, and vanilla. Process until smooth, about 1 minute.

6. Pour mixture into serving dish and stir in chia seeds. Set aside to thicken, about 1 minute.

7. Serve immediately. Or refrigerate 20 minutes and serve chilled.

Hearty Apple Almond Salad

Prep Time: 5 minutes

Servings: 1

INSTRUCTIONS

1 apple

1 small banana

1/4 cup blueberries

1/4 cup raw almonds

2 dried pitted dates

2 tablespoons pomegranate seeds (or dried goji or noni berries)

1/4 teaspoon ground cinnamon

INGREDIENTS

1. Core and dice apple. Peel and dice banana. Add to serving dish and mix to combine. Top with blueberries.
2. Chop almonds and dates. Or add to food processor and pulse to coarsely grind.
3. Top fruit with chopped nuts and dates. Sprinkle with pomegranate seeds and cinnamon and serve immediately.

Spinach Mushroom Muffins

Prep Time: 10 minutes

Cook Time: 15 minutes

Servings: 12

INGREDIENTS

1 cup almond flour

2 eggs

1 cup fresh spinach

1/2 cup fresh mushrooms

1 tablespoon sweetener*

1 tablespoon apple cider vinegar

1 teaspoon baking soda

1 teaspoon baking powder

1/2 teaspoon ground nutmeg

1/2 teaspoon dried basil

INSTRUCTIONS

1. Preheat oven to 350 degrees F. Line muffin pan with paper liners or lightly coat with coconut oil. Heat medium pan over medium-high heat.

2. Slice mushrooms and add to hot pan. Sauté about 3 minutes, then add spinach. Sauté until water evaporates, mushrooms are cooked through and spinach is wilted. Set aside.

3. Beat eggs, sweetener and vinegar in medium mixing bowl with hand mixer or whisk until thick and frothy.

4. Add sautéed veggies, almond flour, baking soda and powder and spices and mix until combined.
5. Use ice cream scoop or tablespoon to pour batter into prepared muffin pan.
6. Bake 15 - 20 minutes, until edges are golden brown and tops are firm.
7. Remove muffins from oven and let cool about 5 minutes.

Tahini Evening Snack

Prep time: 3 minutes

INGREDIENTS

2 tbsp organic Tahini

1 tsp cinnamon

½ cup baby carrots

1 stalk celery

INSTRUCTIONS

1. Slice the celery stalk into small pieces, about the size of the baby carrots.
2. In a very small bowl, mix the tahini and cinnamon together.
3. Serve. Eat by dipping the vegetables in the tahini/cinnamon mix.

Frozen Cashew Balls

Prep time: 15 minutes

INGREDIENTS

½ cup organic cashew butter

⅓ cup flaked coconut

2 tbsp organic maple syrup

¼ tsp cinnamon

INSTRUCTIONS

1. In a bowl, combine all the ingredients and mix well.
2. Separate into small balls and roll them together in your hands. Place the balls in the fridge for 20 minutes, or in the freezer to make them feel thicker.
3. Serve.

Flourless Cocoa Zucchini Muffin

Prep Time: 10 minutes

Cook Time: 15 minutes

Servings: 12

INGREDIENTS

1 1/2 cups almond flour

2 cage-free eggs

1 small zucchini (about 1 cup grated)

1/2 cup unsweetened applesauce

1/4 cup date butter (or agave or raw honey)

1/4 cup coconut oil (or cacao or coconut butter, melted)

1/4 cup cocoa powder

2 tablespoons ground chia seed (or flax meal)

1 teaspoon baking soda

1 teaspoon baking powder

1 teaspoon vanilla

1 teaspoon ground cinnamon

1/2 teaspoon Celtic sea salt

1/4 cup cocoa nibs or chocolate chips (optional)

INSTRUCTIONS

1. Preheat oven to 350 degrees F. Line muffin pan with paper liners or lightly coat with coconut oil.

2. Add eggs, oil or melted butter, applesauce and date butter to food processor or high-speed blender. Process until thick, light mixture forms, about 1 - 2 minutes.

3. Sift almond flour, cocoa powder, chia or flax meal, baking soda and powder, salt and spices into processor. Process to combine, about 1 minute.

4. Grate zucchini and stir in with cocoa nibs or chocolate chips (optional).

5. Use scoop or tablespoon to pour batter into prepared muffin pan. Bake for about 15 - 20 minutes, until toothpick inserted into center comes out clean.

6. Remove from oven and let cool about 5 minutes.

7. Serve warm. Or let cool completely and serve room temperature.

Chocolate Chip Trail Mix

Prep Time: 5 minutes

Servings: 4

INGREDIENTS

1/2 cup raw almonds

1/2 cup raw pumpkin seeds

1/2 cup cashews

1/4 cup golden raisins

1/2 cup organic chocolate chips (or chocolate bark or cacao nibs)

INSTRUCTIONS

1. Roughly chop chocolate bark, if using. Add chocolate or cacao nibs to medium mixing bowl with raisins and nuts. Mix to combine.

2. Transfer to serving dish and serve immediately. Or store in cool dry place in airtight container.

Vanilla Bean Shortbread Cookies

Prep Time: 5 minutes

Cook Time: 20 minutes

Servings: 12

INGREDIENTS

1 2/3 cups almond flour

2/3 cup almonds (blanched, skinless)

1/4 cup coconut oil (or cacao butter or coconut butter, melted)

1/4 cup date butter (or raw honey or agave)

1 Madagascar whole vanilla bean

1/4 teaspoon baking soda

1/4 teaspoon Celtic sea salt (plus extra)

INSTRUCTIONS

1. Preheat oven to 300 degrees F. Line sheet pan with parchment or baking mat.

2. Add almonds to food processor or high-speed blender and process until finely ground, about 2 minutes.

3. Add ground almonds to medium mixing bowl. Sift in almond flour, baking soda and salt.

4. Split vanilla bean pod in half and scrap insides into small mixing bowl. Add oil or melted butter and date butter. Mix to combine.

5. Pour vanilla mixture into flour mixture and mix to form dough.

6. Use mini ice cream scoop or tablespoon to drop portions of dough onto prepared sheet pan. Bake for 20 minutes , or until lightly browned.

7. Remove from oven and let cool at least 5 minutes.

8. Serve warm. Or let cool completely and serve room temperature.

Crunchy Eggplant Chips with Honey

Prep Time: 10 minutes

Cook Time: 20 minutes

Servings: 4

INGREDIENTS

1 medium eggplant

2 cage-free eggs

1/3 cup almond flour (or almond meal)

1/3 cup coconut flour

1/4 cup arrowroot powder

1 teaspoon Celtic sea salt

1/4 cup raw honey (or agave)

Coconut oil (for cooking)

Water

INSTRUCTIONS

1. Heat medium pan over medium-high heat. Coat pan with 1/4 inch coconut oil.
2. Cut off ends of eggplant. Carefully slice eggplant crosswise into thin slices about 1/8 inch thick with sharp knife or mandolin. Sprinkle with 1/2 teaspoon salt.
3. Add arrowroot powder to shallow dish. In separate shallow dish, blend almond flour, coconut flour and remaining salt. Whisk eggs in small mixing bowl or third shallow dish.

4. Dredge eggplant slices in arrowroot, shaking off excess. Dip dusted eggplant into egg, turning several times to coat. Shake off excess and dredge eggplant in flour mixture and coat well. Transfer to large dish for storage between steps.
5. Carefully place coated eggplant in hot oil and cook 1 - 2 minutes on each side, until golden brown and crisp. Turn half way through cooking with tongs.
6. Drain eggplant on paper towel, then transfer to serving dish. Transfer honey to serving dish.
7. Serve hot.

www.ingramcontent.com/pod-product-compliance
Lightning Source LLC
Chambersburg PA
CBHW070112290526
45789CB00005B/2005